Hamlyn all-colour paperbacks

Kenneth Ullyett

Clocks and Watches

illustrated by Martin Battersby

Hamlyn - London
Sun Books - Melbourne

FOREWORD

Horology is a fascinating science with perhaps the longest history known to man. It ranges from the obelisks and sundials of earliest times to the complex timekeeping devices necessary to implement colour television, data transmission and the guidance and control of manned space missions. Here, the intervals of time need to be measured in fractions of a nanosecond, which is one thousand-millionth (10^9) of a second.

Between these extremes of timekeeping, there is an infinite range of clocks, watches, dials, regulators, chronometers, turret clocks and floral clocks. Their interest and appeal include the coldly scientific, the intriguingly antiquarian, the rich jewel, and the modern electronic watch with its buzzing tuning fork making more than 31,000,000 vibrations every twenty-four hours.

There are, of course, many books on horology in general, some with colour plates, some dealing with specialized aspects of the subject, but few embracing the whole scope. This book does so, covering more than 5,000 years and illustrating, as the Book of Wisdom put it, that 'Our time is a very shadow that passeth away'.

K.U.

Published by The Hamlyn Publishing Group Limited
London · New York · Sydney · Toronto
Hamlyn House, Feltham, Middlesex, England
In association with Sun Books Pty Ltd Melbourne

Copyright © The Hamlyn Publishing Group Limited 1971

ISBN 0 600 00289 6
Phototypeset by Filmtype Services, Scarborough, Yorkshire
Colour separations by Schwitter Limited, Zurich
Printed in Holland by Smeets, Weert

CONTENTS

The dawn of time

Astronomers and mathematicians argue whether time exists in the universe or is merely 'relative'. Yet other scientists are striving to perfect atomic frequency standard clocks (devices for measuring this possibly non-existent commodity, time) with an accuracy of one part in ten thousand million, or one second in three hundred years.

This produces contrasts and ironies. For example, on the historic night of 20 July 1969, when the American astronaut Neil A. Armstrong became the first man to walk on the moon, the mission (as with all other major space missions) could be achieved only by precise timing. The Apollo 12 moon landing involved a network of fifteen tracking stations all round the world, and a battery of one hundred computers, representing an investment of more than $500 million. These predicted and united the launching, landing and return with split-second timing in units of millionths of a second. Electronic clocks were displayed on television screens and transmitted micro-second time pulses.

Yet, while all this was happening, radio telescopes on the far side of the world from Houston Control were scanning the outer edges of space, as part of the continuing programme to determine whether man's present understanding of time and space is not confounded by an encircling universe of infinite dimensions.

Extremely complex time-measuring electronic equipment is totally different, of course, from the clocks and watches to be found in almost every home. Space-age equipment makes instant calculations of time-start co-ordinates, of the gravitational fields of the sun and the moon, and of the spacecraft's position, speed and direction at every instant. Yet while astronauts are in flight they check their time and position, taking bearings with instruments developed from those in use more than five hundred years ago, telling the time from the positions of fixed stars.

For many centuries before the advent of mechanical clocks, primitive man could distinguish the passage of time with the

Cast of Egyptian shadow-stick, and water bowls from the Temple of Karnak, dating from *c.* 1400 BC

help of the clock of the sky, his life being regulated by sunrise and sunset. All living organisms settle naturally into a pattern of time. From birth to death, through periods of hunger and gestation, through daylight and darkness and through the ever-changing seasons, everything happens in a sequence of varying duration.

In the very earliest stages of civilization there was no need to record the passage of events with precision, so it passed without notice that in its path across the heavens the sun cast a shadow of varying length, or that a cracked pot cast into the water sank slowly in a fixed duration of time. There were, at first, more pressing things to mark the passing of the day:

When I was a boy
My belly was my sundial –
One more sure
And more exact than any
other.

So wrote Titus Plautus, the Roman dramatist who died in 184 BC. Man's biological and physiological functions marked the passing of time through countless centuries

Melting candle rings mark the passing of the hours

before the positions of the sun and the stars were used as markers of events. Much later, too, came destructive methods such as the burning of a candle or a length of rope knotted at fixed intervals to record the passing of time-intervals.

Earliest civilizations dwelt in areas such as the Nile delta (the Egyptians and Hebrews, Assyrians and Phoenicians) by the Mediterranean, the very name of which means 'the middle of the earth'. Here the seasonal variation in the length of the day is much less than in the higher and lower latitudes of, say, London and New York, or Sydney and Cape Town. In London the length of daylight varies from $7\frac{3}{4}$ to $16\frac{1}{2}$ hours, while in northern Egypt there is only a two-hour variation between approximately ten to fourteen hours. Therefore, as civilization developed in the deltas of the Nile, Euphrates and Tigris, and the Indus basin, it came to be realized that the so-nearly-constant passage of the sun overhead cast a regularly-varying shadow from any tree, tall building or obelisk.

The rate of burning a knotted cord can tell the time

The constant recurrence of these phenomena resulted in 'sun time' being adopted as a measure, at times with dramatic or even historic effect.

The Bible records that: 'Isaiah the prophet cried unto the Lord: and he brought the shadow ten degrees backward, by which it had gone down in the dial of Ahaz' (2 Kgs. 20:11).

'When the shadow is ten steps long, come to dinner,' says one of the characters in *The Frogs*, by the Athenian dramatist Aristophanes (445–380 BC). So deeply ingrained in the nature of the common man did the sun clock become that the Book of Wisdom (2:5) epigrammatized it for all mankind: 'For our time is a very shadow that passeth away. . . .'

A number of obelisks, the world's first clocks, still exist and cast their varying shadows according to the hour of the day. Granite obelisks were erected at Heliopolis ('Sun city') by Thothmes III in 1600 BC as giant sun-markers, and one of these is the so-called 'Cleopatra's Needle' brought to the London Thames Embankment in 1878. In Rome's Campus Martius is the obelisk erected by the order of the Emperor

(*Above*) a nocturnal or night dial, telling time by fixed stars.
(*Opposite*) a 14th-century brass astrolabe, which can show the time by measuring the altitude of the sun

Augustus in 27 BC, still showing the daylight hours as it did nearly two thousand years ago. Far older time-markers are the ring of megalithic stones that form Stonehenge on Salisbury Plain, and the rock pillars in Peru.

In our present age we have the extremes of the countryman marking the passing of time by 'next mucking' (when his land is fertilized), and the scientist seeking measurements of time even smaller than microseconds.

So, at the dawn of civilization, it was inevitable that man should find the lunar and menstrual cycles, or even the regular rotation of daylight and darkness, inadequate. Also it was inconvenient that time could not be marked at night by the length of a shadow or the height of the overhead sun.

The world's oldest civilizations – the Egyptian, Babylonian and the Chinese – had noted that if a stick were notched at full moon, twelve such notches saw a regular rotation of the seasons. From this came the demarcation of time

into twelve 'moons' (the word comes from the Greek *mēn*, month).

We shall never know how many long, dark ages of human progress passed before each 'moon' was split (on a notched stick, or by engraved marks on a stone pillar) into twelve shorter sessions or 'seasons'. (The name 'hour' is derived from the Greek *hōra*, a season.)

More than three thousand years ago the Egyptians inherited the system of a lunar month of thirty days and, as their religion was based on the worship of the sun, adapted this to a solar year. Time was assumed to commence at midnight, in preparation for the glory of the midday sun. The twelve months of thirty days gave a year of 360 days and, to correct this with the solar year of approximately 365 days, the Egyptians added five days named after the birthdays of their great deities – Osiris (god of the underworld, husband of Isis), Horus (god of light, represented by a hawk's head), Set (god of evil, brother of Osiris), Isis and Nephthys.

An even older timekeeping

Egyptian bronze merkhet, inlaid with gold and silver

system, the origin of which has long been forgotten, took sunset as the start of each main division, the period from one sunset to the next being subdivided into twelve, and these subdivisions into thirty parts. This was the fashion for reckoning time-intervals among the ancient Sumerians from whose defeat the Babylonian Empire was founded. By the era of Babylon's famous 'hanging' gardens (terraces), when the Jews were brought captive there by King Nebuchadnezzar, Babylonian and Persian travellers from this area of the Euphrates must have taken this starting-at-sunset time system across the world to China. Japanese time was on a similar basis.

In the high level of Egyptian civilization, great importance was placed on astronomical and astrological forecasts, and devices were developed for telling the time from the positions of fixed stars. In Upper Egypt, in 600 BC, the merkhet (a plumbline) was used to observe the transit of known fixed stars across the meridian, telling the night hour.

Hourglasses, including a set of four for different rates

Sun time

Whether reckoning intervals of time from midnight, as did ancient Egyptian astronomers, or from sunset, as was the habit of the early Sumerians, the night hours were to them of paramount importance. As Shakespeare expressed it, many centuries later:

All the world will be in love with night,
And pay no worship to the garish day.

Elaborate systems were developed for determining the hour of the night, and some of the instruments used exist to this day. For example, in the Cairo Museum is an alabaster bowl water clock found at the Temple of Karnak, Upper Egypt, dating from the reign of King Amenhotep III (1380 BC), and used to show the time during the night hours. In later centuries these clocks were known as clepsydrae (from the Greek *kleptō* to steal and *hudōr*, water). A clepsydra is appropriately named, for there is a small hole at the base of the bowl through which the water is 'lost', and as the level falls the hour can be told from marks inside the vessel. In other types, a pierced bowl was floated inside a larger one filled with water.

There is far more ingenuity here than is obvious from cursory inspection. If the vessel were straight-sided, the rate of water loss would be greater during the early hours of the night due to the pressure of a greater head of water. Markings inside compensate for the larger cross-section of the bowl at the top. Further, there were in practice two different systems of timekeeping in use, and the water clocks needed to display both. Learned men such as the priests and astronomers used 'equinoctial' time, with hours divided mathematically into sessions of equal length, based upon the length of day and night at the equinox – the time at which the sun appears to cross the equator, when day and night are of equal length. Unable to make such a calculation, ordinary people shunned the 'astronomical day', and divided periods of daylight and darkness into twelve hours each. Their clepsydrae and

(*From the top*) Saxon sundial; Flórentine cubical sundial, 1560, showing Italian, Jewish and Babylonian hours; 1574 ivory portable dial by Hans Duche, with a compass to face the dial south

Sundials at Wimborne Minster and (*below*) Morden College

their sundials were required to indicate the 'temporal' hours, which varied from season to season and indeed from day to day. This was achieved in the alabaster bowl clock from Karnak, and in a later white limestone bowl found at Edfu, Upper Egypt (now also in the Cairo Museum), where water trickles *into* the vessel. In both water clocks the inner surface has twelve series of dots marked by the potter, with the name of the appropriate month to which the time-scale refers.

For outdoor use at night, the merkhet and, later, the astrolabe could be used to mark the positions of fixed stars. One of the earliest merkhets is in the collection at the Science Museum, London. It dates from 600 BC, and is an inlaid bronze instrument used by Bes, the astronomer-priest of the god Horus.

In the same museum collection is a Florentine cubical sundial of about AD 1560, showing that, despite the passage of more than two thousand years and the invention of mechanical clocks, many people still tolerated timekeeping systems based on several systems, including the old Babylonian.

This cubical dial (*see* p. 12) is of wood, painted with arabesques, and with short 'styles' (gnomonic spikes, telling the time by shadow) on five faces. Dials on north and south faces indicate Italian hours (the day being divided into twenty-four equal hours beginning and ending at sunset), while the top face shows Babylonian hours, in this case starting at sunrise. The east and west dials indicate the time in the Jewish mode, with temporal hours.

Since the apparent positions of the sun vary according to the latitude of observation, sundials need to be designed for specific use. This cubical dial is for latitude 46°, and was formerly in the Pitti Palace, Florence.

The Greeks devised a complex type of sundial known as the hemispherium, carved from a stone block so that a gnomon shadow is cast across a curved path, depending upon the season of the year. The Chaldean astronomer Berosus created a simplified form of this, the hemicycle, about 300 BC. This was copied widely across Europe in the following centuries. Rome had its first sundial about 290 BC, and religious application was not long in following.

Three sundial styles: (*left to right*) inclined gnomon, modern hemispherium, and hemicycle with pin

Mechanical time

Civilization today has found the key to many secrets, but has lost record of the origins of others. We simply do not know who invented the wheel, or discovered how to extract metal from ore. Nor do we know who made the first mechanical clock. It is impossible to be certain from studying ancient records, because of vague terminology.

Many words were derived from the Latin *horologium*, and in the earliest writings it is impossible to tell if the men of science were meaning hourglasses (sandglasses), clepsydrae, sundials, horacudii (striking mechanisms without dials), or true timepieces bearing even the slightest resemblance to a modern clock.

However, we can be fairly certain that the first major development of the mechanical clock took place in religious communities during the so-called Dark Ages – that is, from the fall of Rome in the fifth century AD to the coronation of Charlemagne (Charles the Great), king of the Franks, in AD 800. In those Carolingian days only the monasteries were safe from marauding tribes of Goths and Huns. Religious houses were havens of security, ruled firmly by time and order, dominated by the canons of ecclesiastical law laid down by the popes. Prayers were regularly chanted at fixed time-intervals, marked by the tolling of a bell. It was an obvious advantage when a mechanism could be invented to ring the bell automatically, and it was then but a short step to adding a dial and pointer to indicate the hours.

A number of important horological developments were made, however, very early in the Christian era. St Gregory (AD 604), who sent Augustine to England, is credited with having set up a clock mechanism. Pacifus, Archdeacon of Verona, and Pope Sylvester II are among other religious figures to whom old records ascribe various *horologia*, but it may well be that Alexandria, in Egypt, was the birthplace of the world's first clock mechanisms, near the beginning of the first Christian century.

(*Above*) fragment from Hero's *Pneumatics*, published in Urbino in 1575, the diagram reconstructed by Frémont in 1915. (*Below*) part of Villard's rope mechanism, 1250

HERONIS

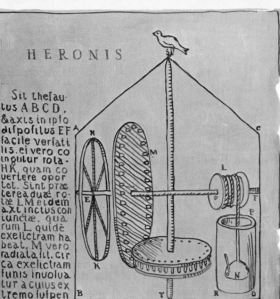

Sit thefau-
tus A B C D,
& axis in ipfo
difpofitus EF
facile verfati-
lis. ei vero co-
ingitur rota
HK. quam co-
vertere opor-
tet. Sint præ-
terea duæ ro-
tæ LM eidem
axi inclufæ con-
iunctæ. qua-
rum L quidé
exellctram ha-
beat, M vero
radiata fit. cir-
ca exellctram
funis involua-
tur a cuius ex-
tremo fufpen-
datur clibanus N, tubum habens XO, & in fummitate fy-
ringulam. quæ melancoryphi vocem reddat. fubijcia-
tur autem clibano aquæ vas PR. & à vertice thefaur.
demittatur axiculus ST. qui facile conuerti pofsit. habet-
que ad Smelancoryphum, ad T vero tympanum radia-
tur. cuius radij radijs tympani M implicentur. contin-
getitur. conuerfa rota HK funemque euoliet
voluj. & c
gravitate
edere. fin
verfione

par chu fait on un angle renu
son doit ader' ueri le folel

Until about AD 600, Alexandria was a famed centre of learning. For some three hundred years of the Alexandrine Age philosophy thrived there, characterized by the attempts to combine Greek philosophy and Christianity. Literature and science flourished. One of the great inventors of the Alexandrine Age was Hero (a man, not to be confused with the lovely priestess of Greek legend, for whom Leander died), to whom is popularly accredited the principle of jet turbine reaction.

Records of his work, in Latin, were printed in Urbino, Italy, in 1575, and a wood-cut of what has since come to be known as Hero's Piping Bird clock is reproduced, with a fragment of the Latin text, on p. 17.

The description starts: 'Let there be a framework A, B, C, D, with a shaft E, F, turning easily . . .' A rope is coiled around a drum Z, supporting a bell-like piston able to drop into the cylinder PR, partly filled with water. As the piston descends, air is trapped and this blows a bird-whistle. At the same time the shaft drives the crude gearing, and turns the bird. The figure depicted is largely a reconstruction of Hero's scheme by the distinguished French engineer Charles Frémont, in 1915. It could not work as described, since if the bell were arranged to fall slowly in the cylinder so that the position of the bird could be used as a time-indicator, insufficient air pressure would be created to blow the whistle. Hero had not, in fact, solved the basic problem of horology, which is to provide a mechanism capable of slowing motion down to a practical 'escapement' of time-intervals.

The diagram below the page from *Heronis* illustrates an early attempt to slow down a wheel mechanism and to provide a recoil, by turns of rope around a shaft on which the flywheel is mounted. The end of the rope is wound on a vertical shaft and terminated by a drop-weight. This mechanism was devised by Villard of Honnecourt, near Cambrai, and was primarily not for an horloge but to oscillate the figure of an angel. The lead figure of an angel, probably operated by a mechanism of

A portrait of Leonardo da Vinci dominates two of his inimitable mirror-reversed sketches, showing one of his many diagrams for a fusee, a pendulum, and a verge escapement mechanism

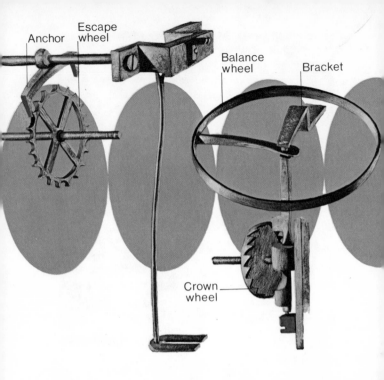

Anchor   Escape wheel   Balance wheel   Bracket

Crown wheel

(*Left*) diagram of an anchor clock escapement, named from the shape of the pallets and pendulum crutch. (*Right*) balance-wheel driven by a vertical crown-wheel

the Villard type, was mounted over the east end of Chartres Cathedral before the fire of 1836. In the British Museum, London, is a record dated November 1344, of a horloge similar to the Villard mechanism, built by 'Walter the Organer'.

By mistake, the early Villard drawing shows the rope coiled in the wrong direction around the flywheel shaft. It was no error, however, which results in many of the notes and drawings of that great genius Leonardo da Vinci being written laterally inverted, so that they need to be studied in a mirror. This famous artist, sculptor, mathematician and composer used this system as a code to protect his private notes and records. In the Leonardo sketches shown here on p. 19, the lateral inversion has been corrected, so it can readily be seen that the sketch on the right is of a pendulum and crutch, and that on the left is of a 'fusee' – a mechanism using a conical wheel or pulley driven from a clock-spring, correcting the physical defect that the force exerted by a spring is not constant, but decreases as it unwinds.

There is no evidence that Leonardo applied the principle of the pendulum to a clock mechanism, but from these and other drawings by him it is obvious that he had appreciated the use of the pendulum as a precise measurer of time nearly a century before 1581 when Galileo observed a swinging chandelier in Pisa Cathedral and wrote philosophically on the same principle. Vincenzio Galileo, his son, put the philosophy into practice after his father had gone blind; unfortunately Vincenzio himself died in 1649 before completing his clock. After

Two forms of anchor escapement. (*Right*) the earliest form, in which the pallets recoil at each swing; (*left*) the dead-beat escapement

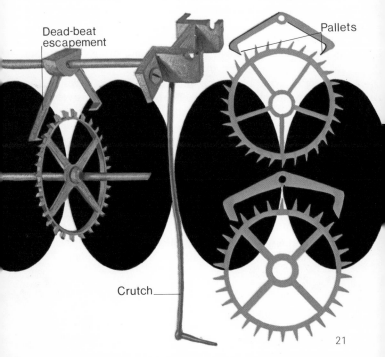

Dead-beat escapement

Pallets

Crutch

his death an inventory was found which mentioned an unfinished clock with a pendulum.

Quite independently, the distinguished Dutch physicist Christiaan Huygens was experimenting with mechanisms for timekeeping, but his approach to the use of a pendulum was very different from that of the Galileos', so there is no hint of plagiarism. On 26 December 1657, he wrote to a friend: 'It was a year ago yesterday that I made my first example of this kind of clock.' On 16 June 1657, he was granted a four-year patent for a pendulum clock, and in time a licence was assigned to Ahasuerus Fromanteel in London.

Long before this, however, mechanical 'escapement' systems had been invented for clockwork, the earliest of which is the curiously-named 'foliot'. This is an oscillating bar, swung back and forth by a wheel with vertical triangular-shaped teeth, known as the 'crown-wheel' from its appearance. The name 'foliot' may be derived from the fooling or dancing motion of the bar, or from the Old French *esprit follet*, a Puckish fairy. We do not now know who invented this, but it has been assumed that a similar vibrating mechanism, driven from a crown-wheel, formed part of a monastery bell-striking train, and that its use for slowing down a weight-driven mechanism for timekeeping became obvious.

Weights were placed on the extreme outer edges of the foliot to control its periodicity. The foliot was extensively used in early clockwork of continental Europe, to the seventeenth century; it continued to be used in many Japanese clocks until the introduction of western time. An advantage of the foliot is that simply by changing the positions of the weights one can correct for the continually-changing length of temporal hours.

Soon the advantage of having a heavy-rimmed flywheel instead of a single bar became obvious, bringing the introduction of the 'balance-wheel' escapement, still driven by a vertical crown-wheel. No reliability of timekeeping was possible with these foliot and balance-wheel escapements.

The medieval astronomical dial inside Wells Cathedral, Somerset, shows moon phases, date, hours and day. Above the dial are automata of jousting knights

24

Chamber clocks

Despite the fact that the clock has become an accepted essential in every home (not yet ousted by telephone dialtime systems or broadcast time signals), the most famous clocks today still include the public, tower or turret clocks, just as they did at the dawn of the monasteries. Millions of people throughout the world know the sound of Big Ben, the bell of the clock above the British Palace of Westminster (the Houses of Parliament), or have enjoyed seeing and hearing astronomical clocks at famous European cathedrals.

Size and complexity of early bell-ringing and timekeeping mechanisms precluded their use in all but religious establishments. Towards the end of the fourteenth century, however, turret clocks began to be seen above castle courtyards and on the towers of other great private dwellings. Where an establishment had an ecclesiastical link, a clock might be built to regulate the ordered lives of the staff. This was so, for example, at Hampton Court Palace, a former priory of the Hospitallers of the Knights of St John rebuilt as a private palace in 1518 for Cardinal Wolsey. There, an inner courtyard is dominated by the dial of an astronomical clock similar to that at Wells Cathedral. After many centuries, however, the original movement (mechanism) was replaced with one constructed by Vulliamy, clockmaker to Queen Victoria.

As the earliest mechanisms were not intended to be seen, they were usually simple frames of wood or iron. Rods and ropes linked the arbors (shafts) supported in these frames with the highly decorative dials, automata (moving figures) or jacks (figures striking bells) above, or outside the building. It was therefore natural that a similar type of construction should be used for the earliest chamber clocks, for use in private homes. An example is shown on p. 24. It is typical of the early great clocks, and is one of the earliest of its kind to have survived. It was discovered by the author, and has been seen by millions of people from all over the world as for nearly a decade it was loaned to the Science Museum, London.

It is a chamber clock, not a turret movement, and presum-

A very early wooden-frame chamber clock, with foliot balance and verge escapement, dated 1643

ably was constructed for mounting in a minstrels' gallery, on the wall of which a dial display would have been painted. The movement has a foliot-bar escapement oscillated by a crown-wheel of wrought iron, but the rest of the motion-work is mostly of wood, with a chamfered beechwood posted frame and arched cresting supporting a bell. The top bar of the frame has the date 1643, the initials 'A' and 'S' (initials either of the owner, or jointly with those of his wife, as in a marriage piece), and the initial 'G' for God – or, more probably, *Gott*, since the clock appears to be from Low Germany.

It is understandable that the first owner of such a clock, with its slow-swinging foliot, would be anxious to show it to his distinguished guests. In the same way the modern owner of a Bugatti or Lamborghini treasures the engineering mechanism under the bonnet, and the owner of a big-screen, solid-state colour television receiver takes pride in the complex array of printed-circuit boards inside the cabinet. Through the

This clock at Rye Church, Sussex, built in 1515, is the oldest in Britain still to tell the time from its original position

centuries, owners of all such innovations have a natural pride albeit a superficial knowledge.

Nowadays only keen antiquarian horologists climb the winding staircases of palaces, towers and cathedrals to inspect turret-clock framed movements; many, indeed, can be seen far more comfortably in museum collections. The oldest turret clock still working in its original position is that at Rye, Sussex. It was constructed in 1515 as a foliot movement, and later converted to a pendulum, the bob of which hangs down inside the building over the aisle. Many other famous public clocks have been restored (as at Hampton Court), and the original movements lost or broken up. The oldest English clock still going, but not in its original position, is that of Salisbury Cathedral. It was built for a thirteenth-century turret in the Cathedral Close, abandoned, and eventually rediscovered by the horologist T. R. Robinson who spent many years restoring it. This turret movement is now installed, working, in the west nave.

Within a hundred years or so of the virtual standardization of turret-movement de-

Movement of the Rye clock, showing separate trains and weights for going and striking

Confector horologij.

Vrmacher.

sign, various centres of clockmaking came into being through-out Europe, chiefly in Germany and Italy where there were already active local industries concerned with locksmiths, armourers and swordsmiths. It was perhaps natural that Augsburg, Nuremberg and other cities where iron-men and damasceners worked should be among the first to produce turret and chamber clocks, using similar foundry and machining methods.

Wooded areas of Low Germany were the natural places for foundries, and in other districts iron ore had been worked from Roman times. Ample supplies of timber were needed for smelting the ore and converting it into malleable iron (with small carbon content) or steel, and for casting it in moulds. Bronze and brass (both somewhat similar alloys of copper and tin) were used by the first clockmakers. Bronze then was an alloy of eight parts of copper to one of tin, and takes its name from the Latin word *brundusinum* (which also means 'brass') from the area of Brundusium where quantities were smelted. Clockmakers' brass (*das Messing*, to the Low German clockmakers) was of rather different composition and colour from twentieth-century machine brass, being an alloy of some sixty-four parts of copper to thirty-six of zinc, with sometimes a trace of lead added to make the alloy easier to work.

Today it is a popular misconception that all early clocks were iron-framed. There is a general term for them – 'Gothic'. This applies to the architectural style of the framework, and is not historically accurate, since the Goths' era began in the twelfth century. Few of these clocks are earlier than the 1500s.

There are several contemporary prints showing how the old clockmakers worked. One showing considerable detail was 'The Clockmakers', in Hans Sachs's *Book of Trades*, published in Nuremberg in 1568. In this can be seen a brick forge, a wheel and other parts presumably for a turret clock, an iron-frame chamber clock, and that prerequisite of every shop in every age – a customer.

'The Clockmakers', from Hans Sach's *Book of Trades*, published in Nuremberg in 1568. A forge is in the background, and an iron-frame clock stands on the counter

Table clocks

We do not know what type of clock Chaucer had in mind, in 1386, when he wrote:

Wel sikerer was his crowyng in his logge
Than is a clokke, or an abbey orlogge

Nor is there any record of the turret clock of which Caxton first printed a reference some thirty years later:

And by this time the horologe had fully performed
Half his nytes cours . . .

Of one thing only can we be certain, and that is both clocks of this period were powered by a falling weight. Earlier 'abbey orlogges' were basically clepsydrae, with a water-driven mechanism sounding a bell at intervals. By the fourteenth century, however, mechanical clocks were almost invariably weight-driven. The coiled spring, known to locksmiths, had not been adapted to drive motion-work.

In 1389 Phillip de Mezières wrote of a noted philosopher and mathematician working then in Padua: 'Known as Master John of the Clock . . . He has made an instrument which shows all the movements of the signs of the planets, with their circles and epicycles . . . In spite of the fact there are so many wheels that they cannot be counted without taking the clock to pieces, all goes with one weight . . . The subtil skill of the said Master John enabled him to make with his own hands the said clock all of brass and copper, without the help of any, and he did nothing else for sixteen years.'

This 'Master John of the Clock' was the famous Giovanni (John) Dondi, born in 1318 in Padua, personal physician to the Emperor Charles IV, lecturer in astronomy at Padua University and in medicine in Florence. Dondi not only built this intricate clock but left a remarkable manuscript in Latin describing every detail of it. At least seven copies of this manuscript were made during the next two hundred years. In our present age the horologist G. H. Baillie made a translation of part of the text, this work being completed by H. Alan

An elaborate Germanic crucifix clock, second half of the 16th century. Time is shown by the revolving ball at the top

Lloyd, M.B.E. Under the guidance of this latter expert, a facsimile of the Dondi clock was constructed by the Clerkenwell clockmakers, Thwaites & Reed, for the Smithsonian Institution in Washington. On the death of Alan Lloyd in 1969, after a lifetime devoted to horology, a fund was raised on both sides of the Atlantic so that another replica of the Dondi clock could be produced, for display in the Science Museum in London. This is perhaps an indication of the importance now attached to Dondi's work by experts of today. Six centuries later we can still regard it to be one of man's greatest early achievements combining science and technology. It was not, of course, a turret clock, but a chamber clock on a stand.

Lloyd's translation shows that 'lantern' pinions (which we associate with early horology) were not used, that all flat sheets were made up from brass, cast and hammered out, moulded parts such as the frame being of bronze. 'Iron' was not mentioned, and even the great Dondi was yet to learn how a clock could be powered by a coiled spring.

We do not know who first devised such a mechanism, but there is in the Antwerp Fine Arts Museum a portrait of a gentleman of the Burgundian Court of the period 1440–50, with a spring-driven clock in the background. It is similar in construction to the domestic weight clock of the period, but has springs concealed either in the barrels or in the thick base of the clock. Above the portrait are two Latin Biblical quotations: '. . . now it is high time to awake out of sleep' (Rom. 13:11) and 'It is the last time' (1 John 2:18), very applicable to the subject although taken out of their context. A portrait of Louis XI of France, about 1475, also shows a small hexagonal spring-driven clock, this time not hanging but on a table.

A weight-driven clock has a relatively constant motive power since the weights fall by gravity. When a coiled spring was used, two enormous difficulties presented themselves. First, there was the problem (still not completely surmounted) of manufacturing a spring which did not break prematurely. Second, a solution had to be found to the difficulty that the force exerted by a mainspring decreases as it unwinds.

(*Above*) clockwork moves this unicorn table clock's eyes and horn. (*Below*) Augsburg table clock, *c.* 1565, with astronomical dials

Lanterns

Augsburg was one of the centres of culture where progress was made in facing both these problems of the mainspring (as the driving spring of a clock came to be known, to distinguish it from other springs used, notably that to regulate the oscillations of the balance-wheel), and some lovely examples of early German clockmaking exist as a perpetual reminder of the glory of Augsburg.

In England, however, the advantages of the spring-driven portable timekeeper were not always felt to be sufficient to outweigh its mechanical disadvantages and fairly poor timekeeping. One particularly charming form of weight-driven construction was the lantern clock, a characteristically English style eventually followed by some makers in Wales, Scotland, France and the Low Countries. It is a posted (pillared) chamber clock, largely of brass, surmounted by a bell which initially sounded as an alarm and did not strike the hours. It certainly does resemble a brass lantern, and was usually designed to hang from a beam. There were spikes arranged behind the rear feet or part of the frame to support the clock away from the wall, as was necessary if a short bob pendulum needed to swing at the back. Some of the very earliest lantern clocks did not have these spikes, since the escapement had a large balance-wheel oscillating back and forth beneath the bell. Hence, provided the bell did not touch the beam there was no need of spikes to support it away from the timberwork of the dwelling.

In time the oscillating balance-wheel gave place to the bob pendulum driven from a horizontal crown-wheel. One form of lantern clock had the striking and going trains between separate sets of plates, with the pendulum swaying inside. Instead of a brass bob, a weight like the fluke of an anchor was arranged to sway from side to side. Glass-fronted and crested wings were attached to the side doors, and in these 'winged' clocks the motion of the pendulum is fascinating to watch.

Relatively few lantern clocks were designed originally to

Fine example of an early lantern clock: 'Jeffrey Bayley at the Turnstile in Holburne Londini Fecit'. It has a balance-wheel and verge, and was made in 1653

Winged English lantern clock, 1660. The pendulum has flukes like an anchor, swaying out into the wings

have separate hour- and minute-hands, although some have been converted. One of the earliest-known English lantern clocks made with a minute-hand is by Peter Closon ('atte Holbourne Bridge, London'), who appears in the records of the Clockmakers' Company from 1632, being senior warden of this guild until 1638. The minute-hand clock probably dates from 1650.

The more usual form of London-made lantern clock is that of the Jeffrey Bayley example shown on p. 34, or the winged lantern on this page. Those on the facing page are Continental specimens (one with the bell removed to show the balance-wheel, and characteristically with a '+' in place of the 'XII' on the chapter-ring, on which the hour-marks were engraved), while the London-made specimens are usually more restrained, better-proportioned and better finished. Dutch, German and Italian clocks continued for two centuries or more in the old style of the iron-frame chamber clock.

Classic proportions of the London-made lantern clock, up to

the mid-1600s, were obtained with a height of usually not more than fifteen or sixteen inches, and a chapter-ring of some six inches in diameter, this ring being seldom more than one inch wide. To some extent one can date this type of clock by the width of its chapter-ring. Up to 1640–5 the ring was thin, about three-quarters of an inch, and the hour-markings delicate. Towards the end of the seventeenth century the rings became wider and larger in diameter. The first lanterns, having only an hour-hand, needed only four marks between the hours, and a simple barleycorn or other half-hour mark. With a single-hand clock it is, of course, very difficult to tell the time more accurately than to the nearest quarter.

When the fashion arrived for a minute-hand, the chapter-ring needed to be wider to accommodate the minute-marks on the outer edge of the circle. The fashion for the single hour-hand continued with country makers until the nineteenth century, and it is a mistake to suppose that all single-hand

Two continental lantern clocks. The bell on the Flemish clock (*left*) has been removed to show the balance-wheel

(*Above and opposite*) night clocks, each with an oil lamp illuminating rotating pierced numerals which appear in turn at the segmental opening in the dial-plate

clocks are of great antiquity. It is difficult for us today to realize how complicated the minute-hand system seemed to our forefathers after many centuries of telling the time from the shadow of a gnomon on a sundial, or from a single hand which bluntly pointed to the hour or to one of the quarter- or half-hour marks. Now that fashionable clocks and watches sometimes display no numerals at all, merely strokes at the familiar twelve positions, the curious fact emerges that people examining an old single-hand clock for the first time experience mental difficulty in reading the time.

Nevertheless, the centuries have made their impact. Children do not take naturally to the concentric minute-hand. Script-writers of farce and vaudeville can still be certain of creating a gust of laughter when a buffoon, on being asked the time, replies hesitatingly: 'Well, the little hand says . . .'

Though crude as is a blunderbuss compared with a fine rifle, the English lantern clock continued in almost unchanging style for three-quarters of a century, with its brass frame, chased brass plates exquisitely worked, and the top three frets carefully cast and filed, usually of a dolphin pattern.

Depending upon the 'fall' (that is, the height of the clock from the floor), the duration was usually thirty hours, during which period a single weight provided motive power for the going and striking or alarm. With some clocks a separate small alarm weight was provided. If the striking train is silenced, by hitching a wheel or putting a wooden wedge in the train, the usual 'fall' will drive the clock for three and a half days as a timekeeper only. Although it must have disturbed the household to have the large bell clanging all through the night, there is no contemporary record of such distress.

In an age when getting a candle lit involved striking a tinder and thus caused difficulty and danger, a non-striking timepiece presented hazards. Of course an oil lamp could illuminate the dial, but the fashion came in suddenly early in

the seventeenth century for night clocks.

It now appears this style first arose in Italy, and it swept across Europe. One of the earliest makers of night clocks was Giuseppe Campani, working in Rome in about 1660. Another pioneer was Pietro Campani. In England, prominent clockmakers such as Henry Jones, John Knibb and the Fromanteels followed the style which has an engraved or painted dial-plate behind which rotates a complex set of hour-circles. These are pierced with numerals, usually tripped in turn by a spring-loaded device and illuminated from inside the clock-case by a small lamp. The piercing is usually covered with silk, and most of these clocks have a religious scene on the main plate.

The night clock on p. 39, now in the Royal Scottish Museum Collection, is by Joseph Knibb, London. The fume chimney can be seen at the top. This clock was originally the property of Archbishop Sharpe of St Andrews, murdered in 1679.

Naturally there is special interest in clocks and watches once owned by famous men and women. The Archbishop Sharpe tragedy helps the dating of the night clock. In the collection of the Worshipful Company of Clockmakers, in London, is a silver watch in the shape of a skull, almost as large as a clenched fist. It is said to have been given to Mary Seton by Mary Queen of Scots just before her execution in 1585.

On the opposite page is an impression of a clock formerly in a corridor at Windsor Castle, said to have been a wedding gift from Henry VIII to Anne Boleyn who sadly could not have foreseen that it would mark the hours of her 'thousand days'.

This precious little clock is ten inches high, just over four inches square, and is of silver-gilt, richly chased and pierced. The Arms of England are held by a lion at the top, while the side engraving features the initials of Henry and Anne, with 'true-lover's' knots. At the top of each is 'Dieu et mon Droit', and at the bottom 'The Most Happye'.

As Harrison Ainsworth commented centuries afterwards, when the clock was purchased for Queen Victoria for £110 5s: 'The object of Henry's eternal love was sacrificed on the scaffold. The clock still runs.'

Richly ornamented weight-driven clock given as a wedding gift to Anne Boleyn by Henry VIII. It was later bought for Queen Victoria

Worshipful Company

Despite a firm grip held on some trades by the rich and powerful guilds, such as the London Guilds of Goldsmiths, Horners, Basketmakers and others, there had always been free interchange of ideas between British and Continental clockmakers. As we saw, a young member of the Fromanteel family was able to work at the Hague for a time in 1657 to glean practical experience in the application of the pendulum to clocks: and one has only to skim through the lists of early clockmakers in London (Delaunce 1650, Seignior 1690, Hilderson 1663 and many more) to appreciate that the workmen whose origins were very probably outside Britain were at first free to work anywhere.

As the demand for clocks grew in London and other cities, British craftsmen became concerned at the influx of foreign workmen. It was an anxiety mingled with religious feeling, during the century or more when Britain swayed between Roman Catholic and Protestant rule, and when the trade guilds began to be fearful of the influence of Rome and the competition of France.

They felt it worrying that an increasing number of foreign clock and watch craftsmen were setting up in London. In 1618 the Privy Council investigated, drew up 'A True Certificat of the Names of the Straungers dwelling with the City of London', and nearly twenty names gave offence. One clockmaker in the ward of Farringdon Within was: 'Barnaby Martinot, clockmaker, born in Paris, a Roman Catholique.' And in Portsoken Ward was: 'John Goddard, clockmaker: lodger and servant with Isack Sunes in Houndsditch: born at Paris, Fraunce: heer 3 yeers, a papist, yet he hath taken the oath of allegiance to the King's supremacy. . . .'

It did not please the London-born guildsmen that foreigners could be free to ply their trade merely by taking the oath of allegiance. It cut right across long-established guild principles of apprenticeship to eventual Freedom.

In the spring of 1622 a petition was drawn up, drawing the King's attention to the 'great number of deceitful tricks' of

Master's Badge of the Worshipful Company of Clockmakers, set against a fragment of the Charter granted by Charles I in 1631

TEMPUS RERUM IMPERATOR

ANNE

Grace of

of England

France & Irela

Know ye that we, at the
of the Clockmakers, as w
freemen of our City of Lor
and inhabiting within the
and suburbs thereof, as

foreigners practising their trade, and begging that they might not be permitted to work except under English masters, and that no more foreign clocks should be imported.

Then, as now, there were deep feelings of labour unrest throughout Europe. It is fair to say the guilds in other cities in Britain were just as harsh to 'foreigners' from outside their boundaries. For example, Joseph Knibb, cousin of the maker of the fine clock illustrated on p. 45, worked for a while outside the limits of the City of Oxford, but in 1667 risked the displeasure of the freemen traders by moving to a shop rented from Merton College. Oxford goldsmiths protested: 'One Knibb, a clockmaker, who is noe a freeman of this City, hath taken upon him to sett up shoppe in this City, contrary to the antient customs and priviledges of the Same, demanding . . . that he should suddenly shutt down his windows and remove either to St Clement's (from when he came) or to some other Place.'

College authorities were reluctant to let the ingenious Knibb family go. Joseph was appointed a Trinity College 'servant' (given the College patronage) to regularize the position, he paid a fine to the freeman traders and stayed in Oxford for two years before moving to London. There he worked at the 'House at the Dyal', in Suffolk Street, for twenty-seven years.

In a city like London, guild problems could not be so easily settled. Master craftsmen had their apprentices to pay, and their families to keep. French goldsmiths and clockmakers ('Catholiques') pleaded with the King in London to grant letters patent for them to ply their trade freely in London, and this is what suddenly brought the fierce opposition of British craftsmen. Until then, most had kept guild status by being associated with one or other of the great City Companies – the Blacksmiths' as a rule. Threat of French competition forced a petition to the King in 1630, as a result of which Royal consent was given to the formation of The Worshipful Company of Clockmakers in August 1631. It continues to this day.

First Master of the Company was David Ramsey, clockmaker to James I and mentioned by Sir Walter Scott in *The Fortunes of Nigel*: 'He mingled his profession with mystical and fantastic pursuits . . . He sold clocks and watches under condition that their value should not become payable till King James was

Rare ebony veneered table clock by Samuel Knibb, from the Ronald A. Lee Collection

crowned in the Pope's chair at Rome.' Guild fears were not without some foundation, it would appear.

Joseph Knibb's famous cousin Samuel Knibb (fifteen years senior) was one of the many distinguished members of the Clockmakers' Company during its first generation, becoming a member of the Company by redemption in July 1663, when he was thirty-eight. He worked for a time in Threadneedle Street, but today his clocks are extremely rare, only five being extant. He had but few apprentices, and one of the most famous was John Miller, whose clocks today are more rare than those of his master. A longcase clock by Samuel Knibb has been in the Royal Collection ever since Samuel supplied it, presumably to Charles II. The cupola-top clock on p. 45 was obviously also made for a patron, but no history of it exists. Mr Ronald A. Lee, the famous antiquarian horologist, discovered it some years ago in South Africa.

Of course, when fine clocks were made for Royalty, each Royal clockmaker in turn found the post extremely lucrative. It is said that Edward East, watchmaker in Fleet Street in 1635, was frequently commanded to attend the King during 'amusements' (such as Royal tennis) in the Mall, when a watch was often the stake played for. The mercurial-gilt table clock by Thomas Tompion, on the facing page, was the gift of Charles II to Barbara, Countess of Castlemaine, afterwards Duchess of Cleveland. Her portrait by Sir Peter Lely, in the collection of the Earl of Sandwich, is famous. The first Duke of Grafton was Lady Castlemaine's son by the King, and this lovely clock has remained in the Grafton family through the centuries. In 1846 the Court clockmaker Benjamin Vulliamy was instructed to overhaul it. He fitted a movement of his own into the mercurial-gilt case, and presented the Tompion movement (at that era an item of historic interest and little intrinsic worth) to the Institution of Civil Engineers, where it has been displayed under glass.

While houses were of lathe-and-plaster, wattle and beams, with low beamed ceilings and irregular stone floors, it was convenient to have a lantern chamber clock hanging by hook

This mercurial-gilt metal-case table clock by Thomas Tompion was a gift from Charles II to Barbara Castlemaine

or stirrup from a beam. Hooded covers were made for lantern clocks, and eventually the whole construction was boxed in to protect the hanging weights and long pendulum. During a relatively brief interim period before the longcase clock and the table or mantel clock dominated the domestic scene, there was the vogue of the hooded wall clock. In Europe the fashion continued right through to the late nineteenth century, with the *comtoises* in France (the zenith of this type was during the reign of Louis XVI), the Black Forest clocks in Germany and the Zaandam wall clock of the Low Countries.

Today some of these have considerable collector's value (for example, there are some fine Zaandam clocks in Amsterdam's Rijksmuseum), but the rarest are those of a handful of London makers.

On the facing page is a fine example by Christopher Gould, an eminent London maker who was made Free of the Clockmakers' Company in 1682. Former great collections such as those of Wetherfield and Pierpont Morgan included specimens of Gould's work. We do not know where he worked, although it has been suggested he was at one period in business with Abel Gould (presumably his brother) near the Royal Exchange. Most of Christopher Gould's work was elaborate, sometimes florid. The hooded clock illustrated here is a restrained, conventional design, with the case veneered in seaweed marquetry. The hood lifts up so that the owner may adjust the hands, but there is no winding-square since the movement is somewhat similar to that of a lantern clock (although 'between plates', as horologists say, and not in an open pillar frame, lantern-fashion) and the clock is wound simply by pulling one of the ropes to raise the weight. At this period, the minute hand was conventional for the more cultured London purchaser. The signature, 'Chr Gould London' is in the English style, not the Latin *'Londini fecit'* (made in London), and the centre of the dial-plate is finely-matted with a punch, not allover, engraved. This clock was made about 1680 and is in mint condition today, apart from some legitimate restoration of the carving.

A rare example of a hooded wall clock by Christopher Gould, made *c.* 1675–80. It has a striking movement and slide-up hood

Tompion is known to have made some of these hooded wall clocks, and so did Edward East and the Knibbs.

A well-known wall clock by Edward East, ebonized, the gilt dial-plate inscribed *Eduardus East Londini* near the two lower spandrels (cherub's heads), formerly in the J. M. Botibol Collection, has fortunately escaped conversion, although this clock is key-wound, with separate going and striking weights, just as with a longcase clock.

As trade in London and the rest of Europe became stylized, to some extent even standardized nationally, many makers became extremely famous, some indeed wealthy.

The Knibb family, Daniel Quare, Henry Jones, the Fromanteels and all the early German and Italian clockmakers have passed on, but the House of Breguet founded in Paris by the great horologist Abraham-Louis Breguet (1747–1823) still produces clocks and watches of the highest calibre. In London, names of great clockmaking families such as that of Frodsham (1781), Dent (builders of the 'Big Ben' movement in 1859) and Thwaites & Reed (founded 1756) live on.

Many horologists have been men of position. John Knibb received the Freedom of the City of Oxford and was its Bailiff and Mayor. William Lee of Leicester (member of a clockmaking family founded by Roger Lee, a Freeman of Leicester in 1691) also served his city as Mayor.

Thomas Tompion achieved fame and fortune in the craft, being in especial favour at the Court of William III. He retired in luxury to Bath, and was eventually honoured by being buried in Westminster Abbey. Visitors to the Royal Pump Room at Bath may see the fine pillar clock Tompion specially designed for Beau Nash in 1706, at a time when the Beau was completing the new Room for his fashionable throng. This clock is nine feet tall, matching the columns of the famous building.

Most of the Royal clockmakers did well, but possibly the largest fortune was earned by John Harrison in the 1700s for perfecting the first reliable marine chronometer. He was paid £18,750, worth over a quarter of a million pounds today.

Three outstanding clockmakers: Thomas Tompion and (*below*) John Harrison and Abraham-Louis Breguet

Wheels and pinions

To old-time clockmakers, their daily life was concerned with what their guild called 'The Trade, Art and Mystery of Clock-making'. The end result was what many people nowadays mistakenly term the 'works', a word which grates on the ears of skilled artificers. The mechanism of a clock is its 'movement', and the trains linking the hands with the driving force (spring or weights) are not made up of cogs and gear-wheels – popular misdescriptions – but of wheels and pinions. Wheels have teeth. Pinions have leaves. They are mounted not on 'axles' or 'rods', but on arbors.

The 'Mystery' of the art of clockmaking has developed its own jargon just as does every other science. Horological terminology is ancient and well-recorded. The curious illustration on the opposite page is from the frontispiece of one of the most valuable and interesting of all contemporary descriptions of clockwork, *The Artificial Clock-Maker,* 'A Treatise of Watch and Clock-Works', first published by the Rev. William Derham, D.D., F.R.S., in 1696.

As the result of valuable recent research by Charles K. Aked for the Antiquarian Horological Society, we now know a great deal about this learned pioneer.

William Derham was a contemporary not only of great men of learning such as Dr Robert Hooke, but of some of the leading London clockmakers. He was privileged to discuss philosophical, mathematical and horological aspects with men of the highest rank, including George II. In his ecclesiastical life he produced books of deep religious feeling which are said to have influenced such other celebrities of the era as Dr Samuel Johnson.

The title *Artificial Clock-Maker* implies a mathematical or theoretical survey of the subject, not an imitation, the original meaning of 'artificial' being 'made by art'. So popular was Dr Derham's book that four editions in English were published, including one in 1759 some years after his death. There were also French and German editions. The drawing on p. 53 did not appear in the first edition. The artist was J. Mynde, but Dr Derham probably provided a sketch which was closely followed. Mr Aked has discovered a letter written to Dr Hans Sloane of the Royal Society, in 1698 (two years after the pub-

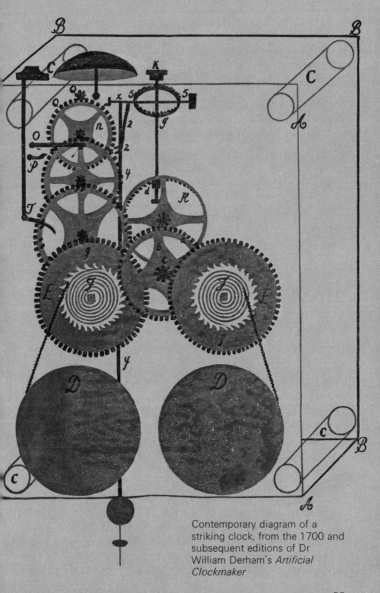

Contemporary diagram of a striking clock, from the 1700 and subsequent editions of Dr William Derham's *Artificial Clockmaker*

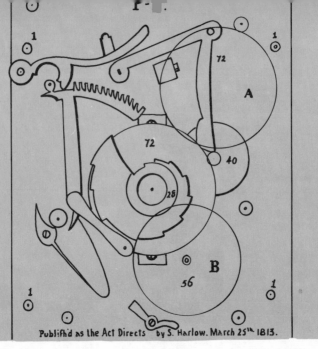

The under-dial motion-work, rack-striking and moon-work of a typical longcase clock in Samuel Harlow's *Clockmakers' Guide*

lication of *The Artificial Clock-Maker*) including a penned diagram of a barometer mechanism, similar in style and lettering to the clock.

Amusingly, in view of Dr Derham's erudite approach to horology, the diagram contains several basic errors. Some years ago Captain W. J. Bentley and I realized that while the illustration gives a good general idea of a clock, with striking and going trains, the latter is shown working in the wrong direction. Later Mr Aked stressed that even this would not make the clock run backwards, as we had at first believed, because the position of the ratchet wheel would not permit the clock to be wound. Further, the going and striking trains are wrongly positioned so that the centre wheel would touch the striking train. And a final error preventing such a clock from working is the positioning of the teeth on the verge crown-wheel. For half the circumference the teeth face in one direction, and in the opposite direction for the rest!

Few heeded these horological slip-ups until the present century. The original E. Chambers' *Cyclopaedia* contained a modified version of the diagram with the same major errors. Nevertheless 'Derham', as the little book has come to be known, is a very fine contemporary account of clocks and clockmakers.

At the beginning of the nineteenth century three major treatises were published, still further expounding the 'Art & Mystery'.

These are Samuel Harlow's *The Clock Makers' Guide* (1813), Rees' *Cyclopaedia* (1819–20), and Reid's *A Treatise on Clock and Watch Making* (1840).

Illustrations on these pages are from the author's photostats of what today is popularly known as 'Harlow on Clocks'. The full title is *The Clock Makers' Guide to Practical Clock Work*

Patterns for the barrel, studs, dial-foot and other components of a typical early 19th-century clock. Birmingham, 1813

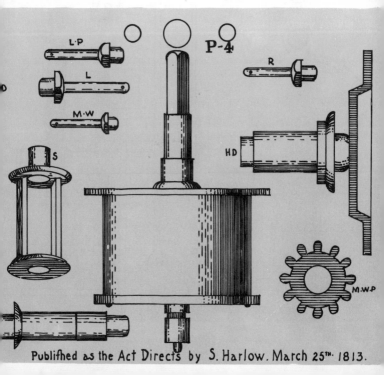

Publifhed as the Act Directs by S. Harlow. March 25ᵗʰ 1813.

with a Statement of Most of the Essential Articles for Making Eight-Day and Thirty-Hour Clocks. Sam Harlow was a Birmingham clockmaker and clock brass founder, and the eleven explicit plates in his *Guide* were from his own pattern-book.

His own advertisement read: 'S. Harlow respectfully informs the Trade that he manufactures Moon Wheels to suit any size Dial, also Caliper Plates correct for Dial Makers . . . also Engines, Lathes, Tools, Files or Materials Proper for the Business of Clock Making'. It is bluntly practical and precise. The extraordinary fact is that although many copies of this pattern-book must have been published from Harlow's workshop in Birmingham's New Street, from his house in Ashbourn, Derbyshire, from two London clockmakers in Clerkenwell and by a London book publisher, it seems that the British

Clockmakers could copy these parts, or purchase components direct from Samuel Harlow who published his pattern-book in 1813

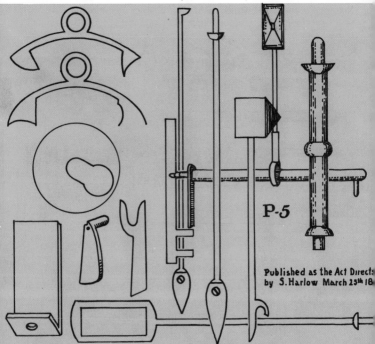

P-5

Published as the Act Directs
by S. Harlow March 25th 18.

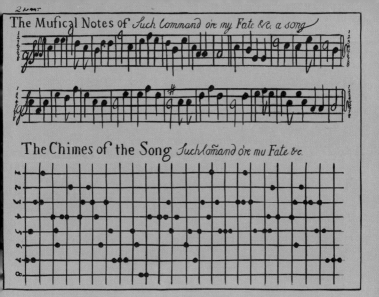

Popular tune chimed out on a 19th-century musical clock, and the diagram used by clockmakers to pin the musical barrel

Museum now has the only original copy extant. Even the photostat copies have collectors' value.

An essential difference between Derham and Harlow is that while the former dealt with clockmaking when it was virtually a new art, the latter, as the expert horological bibliographer Charles Allix has remarked, 'seems to mark the beginning of Birmingham mass-production of longcase movements'.

In 1819–20 followed Abraham Rees' *The Cyclopaedia; or Universal Dictionary of Arts, Sciences and Literature*. This was produced at the time of the dawn of popular education in Britain which led to the rise of the Church Schools. Rees' was the first encyclopaedia to illustrate and detail nineteenth-century technological innovation, with thirty-nine volumes of text and five volumes of plates. He compiled detailed descriptions relating to astronomy, mathematics, mechanics and even subjects such as the (then) advanced one of naval architecture. For the modern reader it is perhaps spoiled by retaining the long-tailed 'f's', which Sam Harlow did not, but the subjects range from clepsydrae to chiming clocks, from dials and dialling to chronometers.

Rees' style is ponderous ('Clock-making, or the art of making clocks, feems not to hold that rank among the mechanical arts, which its connection with the fciences, particularly that of aftronomy, and alfo which the many ingenious improvements it has undergone by the help of fcientific men, entitle us to expect . . .'), but his diagrams are practical, detailed and clear.

Third in this trio of treatises is 'Reid's' – Thomas Reid's *A Treatise on Clock and Watch Making, Theoretical and Practical*. I have a second edition dated 1843, which seems to have followed closely on the heels of the first, and a first edition is almost unknown. There is some doubt about the date of the first edition. Thomas Reid was writing on horology for *Nicholson's Philosophical Journal* in 1805. Reid was a watchmaker, and had the advantage (like Dr Derham) of knowing several of the great makers, while others were still then within living memory. Reid's own claim to fame as a workman was his spring-pallet escapement. It should be pointed out that good early copies of 'Derham', 'Rees' and 'Reid' nowadays have a

Rear view of a table-clock movement by Edward East, showing the bob pendulum (driven by the verge), the count-wheel and vertically-mounted bell

Back plate of a mantel clock by Thomas Tompion, showing pull-repeat levers and bob pendulum

value comparable with that of many an antique clock or watch.

In 1876 F. J. Britten, an enthusiastic horologist, published a little thirty-eight-page book dealing with British manufacturing industries in general, and watches and clocks in particular. It was so well received that he spent the next eighteen years compiling information for a 397-page book: *Former Clock and Watchmakers and their Work*. This was really the first time any competent writer had looked upon clocks as antiques, or upon horologists as craftsmen to be remembered in perpetuity.

The hobby of collecting and studying old clocks then began apace, and in 1899 F. J. Britten produced the first volume of his classic *Old Clocks and Watches and their Makers,* with a list of some 8,000 makers.

Editions grew, and so did the comprehensiveness of the lists. Annie Britten revised the work in 1922, and the sixth, last and best of the 'old Britten's' appeared in 1933, with 12,000 makers listed. During the Second World War vital material was damaged by bombing, and in 1956 a new book was produced under the old title, the joint work of G. H. Baillie, C. Clutton and Courtenay A. Ilbert. The list is now 14,000 makers, but the work is complementary to the older 'Britten's', and in the view of Charles Allix it is desirable to be able to consult both.

F. J. Britten also wrote several editions of *The Watch and Clock Makers' Handbook, Dictionary & Guide* (popularly known as 'the Handbook', to distinguish it from 'Britten's' with the list of makers), the fifteenth and latest edition being compiled by another editor, J. W. Player, in 1955. The illustration on p. 57 is similar to those in 'Reid's' and the 'Handbook', and in this instance shows how the barrel of a musical clock is pinned to produce a contemporary tune.

This is a simple mechanism compared with the complex mathematical deductions necessary to produce astronomical clocks. The basic construction of a clock is not difficult to follow, however, taking Dr Derham's controversial diagram as an aid, or simply from examining the 'works' (movement) of any typical clock.

The driving force is the mainspring, or weight. If there is a separate striking train, the clock may strike the hours only, or plus a single stroke at the half-hour (the fashion in France in the eighteenth century), or perhaps the half-hour sounded out in full on a smaller bell than at the hour (the fashion in the Low Countries and Italy). It may sound the quarters automatically, or when a repeat cord is pulled. Or it may strike a single blow at each hour tripped off from the going train without a separate winder. Or there may be an alarm mechanism, singly or in addition to the foregoing striking systems. If the clock simply tells the time without sounding the hours, it is a 'timepiece'.

Teeth on the barrel engage with a pinion driving the 'centre wheel' via the 'intermediate wheel'. This carries the minute-hand, turning once each hour. There is another train of gearing driving the hour-hand, which of course travels at a twelfth the rate of the minute-hand.

From the centre-wheel there is the 'third-wheel' and finally the 'escape-wheel'.

There has been an enormous range of development in clock and watch escapements through the centuries. The most common is the 'anchor' named from its shape, with entry and exit pallets engaging the pointed teeth of the escape-wheel. In the basic form of clock with anchor escapement there is a pendulum linked to the anchor by a 'crutch'. When we swing the pendulum to one side, a pallet is lifted and the escape-wheel is allowed to move by one tooth. As the pendulum swings back by its own weight, it is kept in motion by the minute pressure of the 'scape-wheel tooth on the impulse face of the opposite pallet on the anchor. This tick-tocking escapement has been the beating heart of horology for over 300 years.

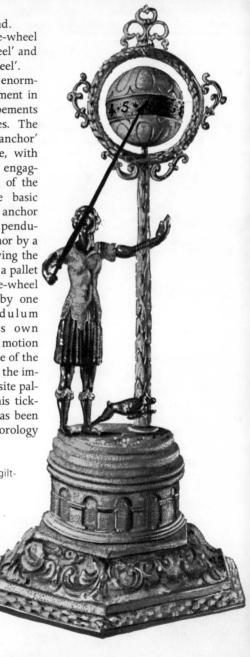

When this 16th-century gilt-metal clock strikes, the figure's head moves and the dog jumps

Although this German table clock was made as early as *c.* 1575, it has a twenty-four-hour dial inside the usual I – XII ring

Watches

In a watch or portable clock, no pendulum can of course be used, since moving the clock would disturb the sway. Nor, for obvious reasons, is it possible to drive the movement by the fall of a weight. Thus, until something more convenient than the force of gravity was discovered as the motive power, there was no such thing as a watch.

This development had to wait until, some time after 1477 in Germany, the mainspring was developed for mechanisms of various sorts. It is possible the early locksmiths pioneered spring development. The horological world has still a great deal to learn about the early years of watches, and all that we can be certain of is that as early as 1525 there were quite extensive groups of spring-driven clock and watchmakers in Germany and France. First horological research led us to believe that one Peter Henlein of Nuremberg was a pioneer craftsman in this field, but now there is reason to believe watches were produced in what is now Burgundy, also early in the 1500s.

Precursors of the watch were the drum-type portable table clocks. The earliest *dated* watch (1548) has a tambour case of gilt metal, but many early watches were spherical. There are examples in the British Museum, in the National Maritime Museum at Greenwich (including a fine example of a French globe watch by Jacques de la Garde, dated 1552), the London Science Museum, and the Ashmolean Museum, Oxford, as well as in many museums and private collections throughout Continental Europe.

While it was not a very complex problem using a coiled spring instead of weights and a rope or chain, the escapement mechanism presented considerable problems – and to some extent still does over four centuries later.

A very early form used a toothed crown-wheel which oscillated a foliot-bar, much

Octagonal watch of the mid-16th century and (*below*) skull watch

Case and dial of a typical watch made in France for the Turkish market

as in the foliot-balance clocks which then had been in use for some two hundred years. Unfortunately this was found to be a very poor timekeeping system. Although the early portable-clock makers were unable to rectify this to any degree, it is much to their credit that they soon discovered the real reasons for irregular rate. The methods they tried were ingenious if frustrating.

As is today well-appreciated by every child who winds a clockwork toy, there is more power in the spring when fully tensioned than when it is unwound. In a watch, the rate decreases accordingly very soon after the wearer winds his watch each day.

A cam similar to those in some early locks was used to help overcome this physical fact, and we can only assume it was a locksmith who devised the method, which became known as the 'stackfreed'. Nowadays we simply do not know whence the name was derived, or whether it was the name of the inventor. In a stackfreed watch there is a spring (sometimes bearing on a roller) bearing against a snail-shaped cam fixed to the mainspring arbor.

Three 19th-century French jewelled watches. The 'touch' watch (*right*) was made by Breguet in 1800

The snail is eccentrically-mounted, the effect being that when the mainspring is fully wound, the pressure of the stackfreed spring resists movement of the snail. But as the mainspring runs down, the force of the stackfreed acts on the reverse curve of the snail, and tends slightly to aid the mainspring. Although it was horologically not very successful, one can only marvel at the ingenuity of the old watchmakers.

On a foliot clock some control of rate was possible by adding or moving weights along the foliot-bar. This could not be done with a foliot-bar verge movement in a portable clock. In some very early movements the ends of the foliot were made to 'bank' against hog's bristles mounted on a pivoted arm. This enabled the wearer to correct his watch throughout the day, closing-up the hog's bristles when he first wound the watch, and slackening them off later. In time a plain wheel was used

(*Above*) French 18th-century watch and snuffbox. Its three dials show hours, days and dates.
(*Right*) watch by J. A. Lepine, with dials showing decimal hour, duo-decimal hour, day of the month and decade

instead of the oscillating bar, but the stackfreed and/or bristle were retained for many years. The fusee, as we saw earlier, was known to Leonardo da Vinci. By the mid-1600s it was commonly used for watchwork, but the necessary length of the fusee spiral precluded any possibility of a thin watch, so many German makers continued to use the stackfreed. The first fusee watches had the spring barrel and fusee connected by fine gut, but craftsmen soon found it possible to make fine fusee chains, and then usually only the cheaper type of watch was produced with a gut line.

Most even torque is distributed between the extremes of a mainspring's wound and unwound state. With the fusee watch, makers found it desirable to get a few turns before the normal winding by the watch-key. Devices were introduced by which watch-menders could put some initial 'setting-up' on the mainspring, using a separate key on a tiny winding-square. A ratchet-and-click system was used at first, then a small worm-gearing to the mainspring arbor.

At first watch-dials were unprotected, like those of table clocks. Later came hinged covers, and after about 1625 glass (rock crystal) was used.

In 1675, nearly twenty years after the pendulum had been introduced for clockwork, an equally important forward step was made with watch design. The Dutch mathematician Christiaan Huygens and the London physicist Dr Robert Hooke both found that timekeeping was improved by using a spiral spring (the balance spring) on the verge mechanism. As the crown-wheel was still at right-angles to the rest of the train, a really slim watch was not possible. In time, however, came the cylinder and lever escapements, and other movements of great complexity and precision. Watches had now begun to take their modern form.

(*From the top*) watch by René Lalique; 1920s watch; 1930s watch

'The Clockmaker's Shop', from a print in the 1827 edition of *The Book of English Trades*, showing a lathe driven by a bow

'Unequality of time'

In 1688, John Smith (one of the early writers on clocks, author of a famous *Horological Dialogues*) produced his treatise on the equation of time: he called it a treatise of the 'Unequality of Natural Time, with its Reason and Causes', and he compiled an equation table: 'Drawn up Chiefly for the Ufe of the Gentry, in Order to their more true Adjufting and right Managing of Pendulum Clocks and Watches'.

Now, the reason why this perplexing matter became a problem towards the end of the 1600s, although known from the fifth century BC, was that only in John Smith's time were clocks and watches such good timekeepers that the sun-dial seemed to be behaving very oddly.

A full explanation of the so-called 'equation of time' is necessarily complicated, but if one refers back to the opening pages of this book it will be recalled that learned men thousands of years ago devised 'equinoctial' time, based upon the length of day and night at the equinox, the time when the sun appears across the equator.

Babylonian astronomers were perhaps the first to realize that the 'solar' day (period between two successive transits of the sun over the meridian) is not regular. Only four times a year does it tally exactly with the 'mean' time of twenty-four hours. While sundials were the only timekeepers, this was not of importance. When the anchor escapement was invented for clockwork, for the first time in the world's history some timekeepers had such a good 'rate' that the difference between clock-time and sundial-time became first puzzling, then a nuisance. Furthermore, it was difficult without a conversion table to set a clock right by the sun.

Sir John Flamsteed, Great Britain's first Astronomer Royal, calculated tables for his own use in 1666 (the year of the Great Fire of London) prior to the building of Greenwich Observatory, and when they appeared six years later in the *Philosophical Transactions*, few could understand them. As a clockmaker, John Smith realized how useful they could be to many owners of clocks and watches. His *Unequality of Natural*

Orrery by Thomas Tompion and George Graham, *c.* 1700, showing motions of the planets round the sun, in relation to time

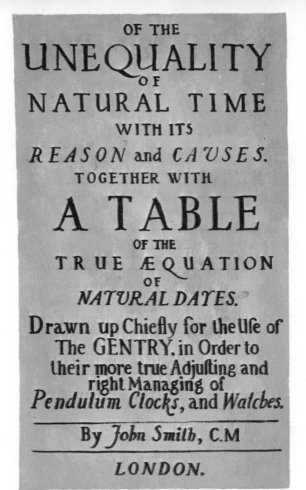

OF THE
UNEQUALITY
OF
NATURAL TIME
WITH ITS
REASON and *CAUSES.*
TOGETHER WITH
A TABLE
OF THE
TRUE ÆQUATION
OF
NATURAL DAYES.

**Drawn up Chiefly for the Use of
The GENTRY, in Order to
their more true Adjusting and
right Managing of**
Pendulum Clocks, and *Watches.*

By *John Smith,* C.M

LONDON.

Frontispiece of John Smith's 1688 treatise on the equation of time

Time dealt with problems arising from the inclination of the earth's axis to the ecliptic, plus the fact that the earth moves in an elliptical orbit around the sun. The four times when solar and mean-time days are equal in length are approximately 25 December, 16 April, 15 June and 1 September. There is not a fixed interval between these dates, nor is there a fixed cumulative daily variation, so the 'equation' is apt to baffle laymen.

Ahasuerus Fromanteel was one of the first to apply the pendulum, and therefore early among those who realized the baffling problem. An ebonized architectural clock by him, of about 1675, anticipated John Smith's complex tables. Fromanteel used a separate minute ring which was a friction fit around the main chapter-ring. Alan Lloyd told me: 'This clock proved a puzzle to all experts for many years, but it is my opinion that the moving ring is to record the equation of time – either by setting the dial daily, or by selecting the apparent time on some forward date, setting the dial to the corresponding equation, and then checking against a sundial on that day . . .'

In the seventeenth century clocks were beautiful, costly, and many gentlemen were as fascinated by the movements of the planets as space-travellers now are in the motion of the moon.

Typical of these leaders of thought was Charles Boyle,

Probably the first Fromanteel clock to be fitted with anchor escapement and seconds dial

Earl of Orrery. He suggested to George Graham, Tompion's partner, that a clock could be devised to tell the time and simultaneously to display the motions of the planets about the sun. One of the finest of these mechanisms, nine inches high, has silver dials and mouldings mounted in a veneered ebony case bearing the joint names of Tompion and Graham. Formerly in the Botibol Collection, it is now in the Fitzwilliam Museum, Cambridge. Many other devices of this sort were made (not all with clockwork), and from the name of the inventor they are known as orreries.

Yet another complication was introduced in the year 1752. By then, clockmakers had realized how simple it was to include a date mechanism, tripped off from the hour train. In 1752 England adopted the Gregorian calendar. This was devised for Pope Gregory XIII in 1582, as a modification of the Julian calendar. For the first time, only the years precisely divisible by 400 were to be regarded as leap years. This brought the civil year into closer conformity with the astronomical.

Some clockmakers issued tables showing the conversion, while others adapted their date mechanisms. One famous clock discovered by Walter Iden is that by John Ellicott, a noted London maker of astronomical clocks. This tall, impressive clock is of one-month duration, and has an astronomical dial display. Let into the trunk door is a subsidiary dial showing the dates before and after adoption of the Gregorian calendar.

Soon after the Gregorian problem had been resolved by Britons, a complexity of quite another sort was introduced by the Government which in its wisdom decided that clocks should be revenue-raisers.

William Pitt introduced a Bill which became law during 1797, providing for a duty of five shillings (then a very considerable sum of money, probably equal to one week's wages for a working labourer) on every clock. Gold watches were taxed at ten shillings, and silver watches at half-a-crown (two shillings and sixpence). The tax could be paid quarterly.

Of course there was a public outcry. Inn-keepers and coffee-house proprietors hastily set up public clocks with

Tavern clock by Dickerson of Framlington, typical of the public clocks in vogue in 1797, when the British Government taxed clocks

THIS WOOD
WAS PURCHASED
BY PUBLIC
SUBSCRIPTION
AS A TRIBUTE
TO THE MEMORY
OF
WILLIAM
WILLETT
THE
UNTIRING ADVOCATE
OF
"SUMMER
TIME"

ERECTED 1927

large painted dials, for the benefit of their customers. The Government soon realized the futility of the Act, and it was repealed the following year. The tavern clocks remained, however, and many larger and more elaborate versions were made long after the 1797 Act was dead. Present-day collectors of antique clocks are apt to group them all as 'Act of Parliament' clocks, however. It has been said that those during the crucial period usually had black dials with painted gilt numerals, and that decorative lacquer clocks or those with white dials are more recent. The 'Act of Parliament' style continued until the 1850s.

Other horological innovations have not had such a swift ride through Parliament. A distant relative of mine, William Willett, founder of 'Daylight Saving', was the great campaigner responsible for many millions of clocks being altered back and forth from 1925 to 1969 until Great Britain abandoned Greenwich Mean Time, Brit-

Memorial to William Willett, pioneer of British Summer Time and the Daylight Saving Scheme

ish Summer Time, Double Summer Time and so forth, in favour of British Standard Time.

Until April 1946, when Britain's Royal Observatory was moved from Greenwich to a site near Hurstmonceux Castle, Sussex, the clocks on which the world's time had been based were housed in the former wine cellars of the Astronomer Royal. Mean Time became Greenwich Mean Time, GMT, and the observatory is still the time centre of the world. William Willett, successful builder, architect, horseman and golfer believed that adherence to GMT robbed millions of people of precious daylight hours. Winston Churchill was among those who backed Willett against opposition and ridicule. In 1925, ten years after Willett's death, the 'Summer Time' Bill became law. One of the factors which influenced Parliament in its decision was the possible saving of fuel for artificial light. The average light in those days cost one-tenth of a penny an hour.

Month astronomical clock by John Ellicott, 1760. It shows dates before and after the calendar change of 1752

Longcase clocks

For the comparatively brief period of a quarter of a century, in all the centuries of London clockmaking, the scene was dominated by a most pleasing fashion, the longcase 'ten-inch' clock. The dial was ten inches wide, generally square. The 'ten-incher' shown on p. 81 is one of the rare exceptions, this dial-plate being ten inches across, and eleven-and-three-quarter inches high.

There is no especial reason why so many London makers should have adopted the ten-inch standard by about 1675. A few Scottish, Bristol and Continental makers at that same time followed the fashion, although their expression of dial design was usually very different. Early ebonized-oak architectural-style longcase clocks variously had dials eight inches or thereabouts across, but there was no standard. At the zenith of the Iden Collection it included Fromanteels with dials measuring $8\frac{1}{2}$ in. and $8\frac{3}{4}$ in., a Knibb (1695) measuring $9\frac{5}{8}$ in., a Daniel Quare (1710)

Early thirty-hour longcase clock by Daniel Quare, 1675, with his first place of business on the dial: 'In St Martins-le-Grand'

$7\frac{1}{2}$ in., and the earlier 10 in. Quare (1675) shown here.

Two very early longcase clocks by Tompion exist, and both have ten-inch square dials. One was in the F. H. Green Collection, a thirty-hour clock with alarm, and a single hand. The earliest key-wound Tompion, shown on this page, was formerly in the Wetherfield and Iden Collections and is completely original. The adoption of the ten-inch standard by the great Tompion possibly induced other London makers to follow, although by the turn of the eighteenth century some makers were turning to eleven-inch and to twelve-inch dials, or even larger.

When Tompion made the key-wound clock on this page he had obviously settled down to few conventions. The duration is only thirty hours (most thirty-hour clocks were wound by pulling the rope or chain, not by winding a key), and as an additional unconventionality the trains are reversed from what had become general by 1675. In the vast

Earliest key-wound longcase clock by Thomas Tompion. Both these clocks have 10-inch dials and lift-up hoods

majority of longcase clocks the striking-train is on the left, as seen from the front. With this particular clock it is on the right. Since the duration is only thirty hours, there is less work for the weights to do than in an eight-day or month clock, and they are less than half the size.

Apart from horological distinctions of this sort, another characteristic which tells us these clocks are early is the style of engraving of the maker's name. With the clocks illustrated on pages 76 and 77 the name is engraved in a scroll ornament known as a cartouche. In the case of the Quare clock his place of business is also shown: *In Martins-le-Grand*. That was his first workshop, and only one other clock extant names it. Long before he became Master of the Clockmakers' Company in 1708 he had moved to premises at the King's Arms, Exchange Alley.

During the 'ten-inch' period, many makers adopted an unusual means for ensuring that no unauthorized servant could tamper with the hands of the clock. In place of an opening door, as was usual with table clocks, the entire hood slid upwards in grooved channels in the back-board. A small curved iron lock, sometimes spring-loaded, known from its shape as the 'spoon', engaged with the lower rail of the hood when the trunk door was closed upon it. Thus only the owner himself, having the key, could open the door and slide up the hood. These details are shown in the illustration on the facing page of a very fine ten-inch clock, eight-day movement with count-wheel striking and alarm, by Joseph Windmills. This is typical of best-quality London clocks of the 1680–90 period.

Usually the 'ten-inch' case was about 6ft. 6in. or so to the top of the cornice. It stood on a plinth or on bun feet. If the top of the hood was not in the architectural form, as in the case of the Fromanteel on p. 71 or the Quare on p. 76, then it might be decorated with a cresting (as is the Windmills, and also the clock on the following page), or with a so-called caddy top built up of concave- and convex-section mouldings.

The hood of this late 17th-century English longcase clock cannot be lifted until the trunk door is opened to release the 'spoon' lock

Because of depredation caused by wood-worm or the death of an old fashion, many of these original crestings and tops have gone. Original crestings were usually of Italian walnut, deeply carved in the design of a scrolled pediment centering in a shell or a Grinling Gibbons' style of cherub's head. London-made cases were almost invariably of oak, veneered perhaps with ebony, later with walnut. Banding, stringing and floral marquetry were conventional. Many great clockmakers patronized the same casemaker. An odd fact is that although clock case making must have been a major London industry, we know very little about these artificers. Nor, for that matter, do we know many of the names of the pattern-makers and brassfounders who provided the blanks for wheels and brackets, or those delightful corner spandrels on dial-plates. We know Samuel Harlow, of course, but he was a Birmingham man, working nearly two centuries later.

Signatures on chapter-rings

Longcase clock by John Ebsworth, *c.* 1690, with pierced hour-ring on a brass dial

and dial-plates were not in the handwriting of the clock-makers, but were stylized by engravers. This we can tell, knowing the signatures of clockmakers from their letters and wills. They were the maestros. The pattern-makers, engravers and the case-makers were anonymous craftsmen, their names now forgotten for ever.

Most of these 'ten-inchers' had 'royal' or seconds pendulums, 39·139 in. long, beating once every second. Some makers experimented with 1¼-sec. pendulums, 61·15 in. long. Such clocks are rare and very valuable today.

As the years rolled on, much furniture became impressive rather than simply utilitarian. With brick construction of houses, living rooms were larger, higher. It became fashionable, particularly in the Midlands and North of England, to have clock cases of monstrous size, with thirteen- or even fourteen-inch-wide dials. Dutch taste went for the *staande klok* half again the height of a man.

This rare Thomas Harris clock has a 1¼-second pendulum

Europe in fashion

While the craft of clockmaking in Britain was dominated by the Worshipful Company in London, and by guilds in other cities, the leading makers on the whole were not prominent in constructing turret or other public clocks. Langley Bradley built turret movements for St Paul's Cathedral and other London churches. Thomas Harris built the 'Gog & Magog' clock for St Dunstan's Church in London's Fleet Street. The Knibbs and their apprentices were responsible for some fine turret clocks in and around the City of Oxford. Wadham College boasted the best Knibb turret movement until 1870, when the College authorities decided it was worn out, and bought a new one for £55 from Dent & Co., makers of the 'Big Ben' movement in London.

Thus the London makers were a tight-knit community, disciplined by the regulations of their Company (liable to be fined for inferior work, or for taking on too many apprentices), and not inspired by the work of makers of 'great' or turret clocks.

It was quite different on the Continent of Europe. Research was carried out by the Oxford historian and horologist Dr C. F. C. Beeson, DSc (Oxon), as a result of which we know that monastic alarms were in use in Germany in 1304, and that there was a public clock at Milan's St Eustorgio Church in 1309. A clock and a bell were made for the Palace of the King of Aragon at Perpignan in 1356. In 1379 this monarch presented his daughter with a small alarm clock: '. . . having three bells and an astrolabe dial showing the zodiac, sun, moon and fixed stars, and with plates adjustable for any latitude in the Kingdom of Aragon'. The general situation in Europe, historically, was that France had been invaded by the Black Prince (1356), and when John II, King of France, had been defeated at Poitiers, the Popes left Rome and took refuge in the Royal Palace of Avignon. Clockmakers continued in their trade, especially the makers of public clocks, and today we know a good deal about their craft from an account book left by Anthony Bovell, *plomberius* to Pope Innocent VI at

French provincial *comtoise* hanging clock, First Republic period. It has an enamel dial, iron-frame movement and verge escapement

Avignon. Dr Beeson's investigations show that Bovell took a staff of ten clocksmiths to Perpignan when bells were being cast and a great new clock constructed.

In England, Edward III inspired architects, cathedral builders and craftsmen in many trades. As early as 1350 there were striking clocks in Windsor Great Tower, at Westminster, Sheen and elsewhere. But it cannot be held that these turret clocks inspired the clockmaking guilds in connection with domestic clocks, as was the case in Europe itself.

In Germany, France and Italy, the fashion for the basic 'Gothic' iron-frame clock continued for centuries, taking a direct inspiration from tower-clock construction. Early English clockmaking developed its own individual line without much benefit from the locksmiths, bell-founders or goldsmiths. Until the London makers formed their own guild Company, many had been members of the Blacksmiths' Company, but we have only to examine many brass lantern clocks and early table and longcase clocks extant to see how the English makers retained an individual approach to the 'Mystery'.

Chapuis records that there was a public clock atop the Cathedral of St Pierre, at Geneva, prior to 1419, when a record of that year names Etienne de Vuy as 'Rector of the Clock', and as a *faber*, or blacksmith. A few years later another artisan, Master Claude Noyon, was appointed *serrallious et magistro horologii* (locksmith and master of the clock), and paid 200 florins for repairing it.

If the locksmiths and blacksmiths were among the first clockmakers and menders in Continental Europe of the early fourteenth century, goldsmiths were in business at least a century previously. Goldsmiths were entrusted with the minting of coin. They employed lapidaries and *cristalliers*, as well as workers in enamel. With the development of the smaller chamber clock, it was natural the trade should move away from blacksmiths to goldsmiths. The need to fabricate small clock, table clock and watch parts in brass and bronze was also instrumental in giving work to the houses of the goldsmiths,

Ornate mantel clock of the Louis XVI period, when such mystery clocks were popular. Time is shown by lifting the figure's eyelids

A table clock by Peter Visbach, of the Hague, now in Amsterdam's Rijksmuseum. It has an ebonized case and a pierced hour-ring showing the velvet-covered dial-plate beneath

because in many European areas there had been bronze foundries from Roman times.

From its relative isolation at that period, England developed along different lines. There were difficulties, risks and delays in carrying clocks by windjammer to French and Dutch coasts (although, as we shall see, within a century or two there was a thriving trade with the Orient; cases were even shipped out to the Far East to be 'japanned' and lacquered), but throughout much of Europe there was a free interchange of ideas and of trade. In the fourteenth century Geneva was holding seven Great Fairs every year. France saw her first Fair at Lyons, in 1462, under the patronage of Louis XI. There is little new about international trade conventions.

While the locksmiths had been willing to work for the average rate ('six sous a day, a meal and free wine', in 1350), and did not set the building of a tower clock on a more costly scale than the building of the tower itself, the goldsmiths felt it necessary to introduce restrictive practices. As in all guilds, young men had to face apprenticeship before becoming journeymen and then masters of their craft.

Thus, except in certain important areas such as the Swiss watchmakers who developed from the goldsmiths, the latter began to price themselves out of reach of potential private owners of chamber clocks. Since they made precious items and ornaments for men of power and for leaders of fashion, the goldsmiths were possibly more subject to the lawmakers' edicts.

At the time of the Reformation, Calvin caused the Swiss General Council in 1541 to introduce regulations governing daily life at any point where it touched upon religious belief. Thus, the laws introduced over a twenty-year period prohibited the making of crosses, chalices and 'other instruments serving for Popery'. Fortunately this edict did not apply in Germany and Italy, where craftsmen continued to produce the delightful Augsburg-style crucifix table clocks.

Gothic chamber clocks continued to be made throughout Europe from the 1500s to the late 1700s, despite the complete change introduced during the Renaissance period. Nuremberg was the leader of style and of craftsmanship, particularly since 1565 when a group of clockmakers rebelled against the rules

This ebonized table clock, made in Vienna for the Turkish market, has Turkish hour numerals, but Arabic numerals on the calendar circle

of the blacksmiths' guild and obtained the consent of the Town Council to set up on their own. They had to produce their own patterns for casting, and design and fabricate their own wheelwork with help from any other metalworkers.

What tricks and devices they did borrow from other craftsmen, however, were virtually common knowledge at the time. This resulted in most Nuremberg-style clocks being rich indeed. An example is 'fire-gilding', known from the pre-Christian era. Mercury has the curious property of forming an amalgam with gold. It was an early device of goldsmiths to make such an amalgam, coat it on chased or otherwise decorated brass, copper or bronze surfaces, finally driving off the mercury in a furnace. A firm deposit of virtually untarnishable gold was left after this firing. The fumes during the process are poisonous, and even expert clock-restorers today eschew this method of gilding dials and cases.

This type of clock decoration reached its peak in Augsburg and elsewhere during the Renaissance, but some of today's most highly-prized clocks are of an earlier period. In particular there are the wrought-iron chamber clocks by members of the Liechti family of master clockmakers, in Winterthur. They were locksmiths who became clocksmiths, mostly in the 1570s and 1580s. Erdhard

Clock by J. M. Jùntes of Amsterdam. Its musical movement has six tunes, chosen by moving the dial arch pointer

Liechti was a leader of the Gothic iron frame and gaily painted dial fashion. Laurentius Liechti also produced many small chamber clocks, but is perhaps best remembered now for the turret clock he constructed for the *Frauen Kirche* (Lady Church) in Munich.

Many a Liechti clock was known as a *Kunstuhr* (that is, a clock regarded as a work of art), and this is confirmed by present-day saleroom values. At auction, on the very rare occasions when a genuine Liechti is offered for sale, it is quite likely to command a figure greater than the total earnings of the Liechti family during their combined lifetime.

While the seas separated Britain from southern German competition and the German workshops of the Schmidts, the Karolis, the Mullers, the Augustas and the rest, there was very little progress in France and Italy.

Eventually the German guild restrictions smothered the industry, and other countries came into their own. As Winthrop Edey, an expert on horology in France, has rightly pointed out: 'The guild regulations that had made German clocks preeminent in the sixteenth century caused the downfall and virtual extinction of clockmaking at the end of the seventeenth, because German clocks remained of a costliness that prevented competition with the more streamlined products of England and France. . . .'

A sad fact is that few very early French clocks have survived. This is because there was no guild of clockmaking in France until 1544 (in Paris), and the goldsmiths had allowed earlier clockmakers to use rare metals. In more modern times the solid silver and gold cases were melted down, regardless of horological interest.

Only seven clockmakers signed the application for a guild in Paris. In Blois, the other major centre of the craft, there were but four makers. Within a hundred years there was a spate of members, together with those forming and joining allied guilds such as the bell-founders, enamellers, casters, chasers and gilders, and of course the cabinetmakers: these were not members of a separate Livery in Britain, where clock-case

Unusual French-style hanging clock with Swiss-type movement giving a bird's song at the hour. A mechanical fountain also plays

Movement of a Catherwood clock, which plays a minuet, a cotillion and a gavot

makers were probably members of the Carpenters Company.

The panorama of all Europe tended to be dominated by the state of affairs in France. So far as horology is concerned, the relative periods are: *l'horloge gothique, l'horloge Renaissance* (in France this comprised the entire sixteenth century), the style of Louis XIV (1643–1715), the brief Regency (1715–23), the style of Louis XV (1723–74), a transition of fashion between Louis XV and Louis XVI (1750–90), when a more severe classic style was in vogue, the so-called *'Directoire'* era (1795–99), the 'Empire' style of 1800–30, and finally the styles of Louis-Philippe and of Napoleon III (1830–70).

The French Empire period began with the *'Consulat'* (1799–1804), and progressed without much change so far as stylish domestic furnishings were concerned through the reigns of Napoleon I (1804–15), Louis XVIII (1815–24), and Charles X (1824–30).

Clocks, in common with other furnishing items, were dominated by the thinking of contemporary Empire painters such as Charles Percier (1764–1838) and

Pierre-François-Léonard Fontaine (1762–1853).

Horologists unfamiliar with the French scene are apt to make quite surprising mistakes – for example they may date the Neuchâtel *pendules* 'early' because they are housed in black cases (sometimes relieved with gold lining), and may regard Boulle ('Buhl' to the Germans) as late because it is delicate and complex. In fact the reverse is true, for the *pendules Neuchâteloises* with their stark black cases and severe white enamel dials were produced until the nineteenth century. And clock cases decorated in the manner created by André Charles Boulle date back to the 1660s and the Louis XIV era.

Boulle-work is a fine development of the art of wood marquetry, which was developed in the Low Countries and brought to a fine art in London – particularly for longcase clocks – between 1660 and 1750.

The art of Boulle decoration for clockwork reached its

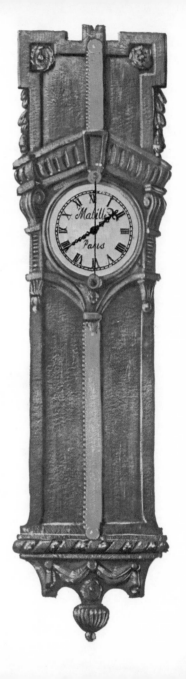

Spring-driven rack clock by Mosbrücker, *c.* 1780. The clock climbs up the rack, unlike others of the type, which fall by gravity

A 17th-century copper-gilt Augsburg clock. The silver dial is supported by a griffin whose beak and wings move at the hour

zenith in some of the fine examples which today are not in their native France, but in the Wallace Collection at Hertford House, London. Mr. F. J. B. Watson, FSA, of the 'Wallace' has made painstaking research into the methods used by Boulle and his craftsmen, as a result of which horologists are now much better informed about French clock cases.

Unlike salon cabinets, clock cases are generally veneered with small areas of Boulle. The base is plain oak, or some ordinary wood such as coromandel. Gilt bronze or ormolu mounts are used at the corners, to conceal joints between sections of the veneer; finials and other solid cast decorations are used, toning with the brass sheet which forms part of the Boulle pattern.

The technique is similar to that of marquetry in wood, thin layers of brass and tortoiseshell being placed together, topped with a paper pattern and cut through with a fret-saw. When the cut layers are separated, it is possible to reassemble them in two different ways – that is, either by inlaying the brass into the shell, or vice versa. French craftsmen described the pattern of brass on a ground of shell as the *première-partie*, and the alternative as the *contre-partie*. To avoid waste of time and material, at least two sets of patterns would be cut at once, in order to produce matching sets of veneers, today known as 'Boulle' and 'reverse-Boulle'. Contrasting pairs of cabinets are known (there are several in the collection at the Palace of Versailles), but it is almost unknown to come across fine-quality 'Boulle' and 'reverse-Boulle' work in clock cases, chiefly because in the smaller areas of such cases a number of small sections of veneer is involved.

On earlier cases the colour scheme tended to be brass on a black ground, but by the nineteenth century case-makers were using horn stained in various colours, or a layer of red or green foil.

Many French clocks today are described simply as 'Boulle clocks', although André Boulle was no more a clockmaker than he was inventor of the inlaying technique for cabinetwork.

As the style developed, the many craftsmen following the Boulle fashion were influenced by cabinetmakers, designers and architects, among whom were Charles Cressent, J. A. Meissonnier and Gilles Marie Oppenord. They moved away from the arabesques and restrained baroque forms which characterized the earliest Boulle cases.

Little is known of the guild restrictions on London case-makers, but the various sections of French case-work and cabinetmaking were strictly regulated by different guilds, such as those for the *ebénisterie* (woodwork) and the *fondeurs-doreurs* (cast mounts).

French clock case styles were widely imitated by Italian, Swiss and Austrian clockmakers, and nowadays it is hard to affirm who may have been responsible for introducing novelties. There was a period throughout much of Europe, from about 1650 to 1685 when the dial-face was covered with red or black velvet, or even chamois leather. Dutch makers used this device effectively, with chapter-rings pierced and cut away to show the velvet or leather beneath. In a few examples it was a style copied by London makers. And it was also used by leading clockmakers in Paris for clocks of the *tête de poupée* (doll's-head) style, so named because the movement is contained in a large and usually semi-spherical case on a larger base, the whole decorated in the Boulle manner. The figure of Chronos, god of Time, was frequently used as a motif

(*Above*) Abraham-Louis Perrelet of Neuchâtel in his workshop
(*Left*) a rolling clock, probably French. As the clock slowly moves
down the slope, the force of gravity operates the train

among the ormolu mounts on clocks of the period, this fashion
starting in the Louis XIV era if not earlier.

Dark pearwood and ebony had been favoured by the Court
of Louis XIII, and in clocks this produced domestic items of
severity, with the numerals on a pewter chapter-ring. They
became known as *pendules religieuses*, going out of fashion in
France with the changes of taste and style coming from the
influence of the Roi Soleil. Even the pendulums of many
clocks of the Louis XIV era have the bob cast in a pattern of
the sun's rays, in honour of the Sun King.

Nevertheless, the 'Religieuse' style was pleasing. To many
discerning people the passage of time is best displayed by an
instrument of neutral severity, just as a grand piano is more
fitting for music than a garish juke-box. In France the sudden
blossoming of Boulle and ormolu produced an entire reign

of gay clocks until the advent of *le style Directoire* (the Messidor period) in the 1790s. Gaiety disappeared almost entirely with the Empire fashion, particularly under the influence of Abraham-Louis Breguet (1747–1823), Lepine, Ferdinand Berthoud and other makers who put horological precision and ingenuity first.

In the Low Countries the peak of influence was seen in the era of the Amsterdam and the Hague makers soon after Huygens. It is in some ways sad that the rich patrimony of the Amsterdam merchants, with their luxurious houses along the canals, did not inspire Netherlands horology to a higher state of art in the eighteenth century.

Of course there were domestic clocks of great ingenuity produced in the Netherlands, including astronomical, organ and other musical clocks. But the standard of workmanship and precision was not equal to that of the French. In Italy, too, the fashions were usually only a poor copy.

Early Dutch mantel and night clocks show good craftsmanship, and today are rare and costly. In later clocks there was obviously no intention to aim for longevity.

(*Above*) this Sèvres porcelain lyre clock, with ormolu mounts and an enamel dial surrounded by brilliants, is said to have belonged to Marie Antoinette. (*Opposite*) a Louis XV-style bracket clock by Bastian of Paris. It is now in the Victoria and Albert Museum collection, London

(*Below*) a synchronizer by Breguet, 1814, designed to wind and correct a pocket watch from a chronometer. It was made for the Prince Regent and is now in the Royal collection. (*Opposite*) regulator clock by Thomas Wright, watchmaker to George III

Unbushed iron plates were used for movements and the brasswork was often crude. In some musical clocks even the pinned barrels were of wood. Few have survived.

The standard domestic clocks in the eighteenth century were the *Amsterdammertjes*, small hooded wall clocks with a short pendulum concealed inside the case, the weights hanging outside. Nevertheless, in Amsterdam there were a few horologists aware of Paris fashion. Nicolass Weylandt headed those clockmakers able to produce a good 'Consoleklok' in the gay Louis XV Boulle style. Movements of the very few such clocks extant show a Dutch influence in the complex dial-work, showing date and moon-phases, although one suspects the Boulle-style cases are French-made.

It has always to be remembered that in clock cases the maker was not leading a fashion, but supplying a demand. When even the walls and floors of French mansions were decorated in Boulle (there is a Boulle inlaid floor, still, at the Château de Maisons-Lafitte), then naturally clocks were produced in a matching style. In countries where life was sterner and in cities of less luxury or under a different religious influence, styles were primitive and austere.

For these reasons the style of the 'Religieuse' was favoured by the Swiss (especially the Bernese) and in parts of Italy, long after it had gone out of fashion in France.

Even in France, by the middle of the nineteenth century there was a drift back to the 'old black ebony'. It was the same in London, too, especially where fine precision clocks were concerned, such as the dead-beat-escapement regulator by Thos. Wright, seen here. Neuchâtel craftsmen revived the ebony style, although continuing the Louis XV balloon lines and matching brackets. The clocks now had bold white enamel dials and gay ormolu enrichments on the ebony. The pretty conceit then in fashion was the use of tiny gilt suns mounted on blued-steel hour- and minute-hands, about half way along their length.

These *Pendules Neuchâteloises* were sometimes fitted with several concentric hands, perhaps one to indicate the date, or for alarm-setting, so it was convenient to have the miniature suns on the two hands which told the time.

French clockmaking has been as closely associated with Court life as it has in Great Britain. Louis XVI and two of Britain's King Georges were deeply interested in horology and scientific instruments. Dr Demainbray started a fine collection of scientific instruments, still preserved almost in entirety, for King George III (1760–1820), and George IV (1820–30) personally supervised a pictorial inventory of clocks in the Royal collections at Buckingham Palace and Windsor.

A probable reason for the generally high standard of all horology in France is this same Royal link, and the position of selected clockmakers at Court.

It was the accepted order to appoint *Horlogers du Roi* (Clockmakers to the King) who worked at Versailles and the Louvre. Originally three makers were given this honour at a time, but later the number must have been extended. It also included clockmakers known as *Suivant à la Cour*, men who (particularly during the reign of Louis XIV) were allowed to travel with the Court. In due time the honour was combined with that of *Horloger du Roi*.

Of course, one should distinguish between *horlogers* of the calibre of the mathematician-horologer Breguet and those earlier men who were little more than *valets de chambre* to the kings. They had the freedom of the royal bedchamber to wind clocks, just as did the wigmaker, the barber and the other palace servants to attend to their respective duties.

Because of the high standard set by French makers, their cases and movements were used in other European countries. English movements are found in Boulle cases and French movements formed the basis of some clocks sold by London factors. In the late Victorian era, the factory-produced high-grade French eight-day movements were widely used in this way throughout Europe.

It was the Empire period (1800–30) which first saw the delicate precision watches, including *pendulettes* (travelling portable clocks of the type now known as 'carriage' clocks) and movements with complex astronomical displays.

Mantel projection clock, popular in the early 19th century, with a metal case, japanned red. Lens at the rear projects an image of the time on the wall. This rare example has an English movement

To the Orient

Clocks and watches rank among the world's first important international exports. As we have just seen, first-quality French cases and movements went out to many other countries. London had a thriving export trade to Turkey. Clocks taken to the Far East by Dutch traders were no doubt instrumental in bringing mechanical timekeeping to Japan and China for the first time except, of course, clepsydrae. China discovered gunpowder and the practical use of lenses, but it seems she made no advance in telling the time beyond sundials and water clocks. Although many European countries exported to the East (there is a Turkish watch made in Paris illustrated on page 64, and an Austrian table clock made for the Turkish market on page 88), there was a high standard of instrument-making existing in the East in the seventeenth century.

As so many clocks and watches exported from Europe to Turkey are florid in style, to the point of being gaudy, and in so many instances devoid of horological novelty (except for the ability of musical clocks to twang out tunes now not recognizable to Western ears), the mistake is made of overlooking the true position. Turkey's former marine greatness, both in the Black Sea and the Mediterranean, had extended to the making of optical, navigational and similar instruments. Astrolabes and even watches actually made in Turkey were the equal of any made in Paris or London at that period.

Horologists seem to have forgotten a great deal about our former Turkish trade. As the author Desmond Stewart once put it, 'Turkey's past is a palimpset – a slate written upon and repeatedly erased through the centuries.'

Nowadays we are apt to describe the indications upon the chapter-ring of a clock for the Turkish market as 'Turkish' numerals. They are, in fact, Arabic. The Arabic script was in use until Kemal Ataturk introduced a Latin alphabet in 1928. It is perhaps fortunate that Islam and the Ottoman State were willing to accept the Western mode of telling the time. The twelve Arabic stroke-like numerals fitted exactly around the

Clock signed 'George Prior', with Arabic numerals and a marine scene. This clock is similar to many Prior exported to Turkey

hour-ring in the positions familiar to those in Europe using Roman numerals on dials.

Until recent years, Turkish-style clocks and watches did not enjoy high saleroom prices among collectors. It now seems obvious that many have been converted to European-style numerals. Moreover, because of the fighting between Islam and Christianity throughout the seventeenth and eighteenth centuries, the export trade to Turkey was some-times halted. At one period, in 1683, the Sultans had con-quered through the Balkans as far as Vienna. Rival armies fighting to establish a frontier were not helpful to trade. Clockmakers in London and other cities suddenly found them-selves with stocks of 'export rejects'. In some cases dials may have been changed to the European pattern; but because the actual position of the numerals is identical, some were un-changed. From the relatively pristine condition in which so many 'Turkish' clocks and watches are now found, it seems obvious they never made the journey to and from the East.

It was not until long after the reign of Suleyman the Mag-nificent – indeed, not until the middle of the eighteenth century – that regular Turkish trade became established, and the old threat to peace in Europe was forgotten.

An interesting horological reminder of the Ottoman Em-pire's final assault upon Vienna came to light through an accidental discovery relating to a Turkish watch in the collec-tion of the Austrian War Museum. Professor H. von Bertele examined this early silver watch, with its complex calendar movement, and noted the positions of the hands indicating the day, month, year, and of course the hour. It appeared certain that this watch (probably made by a European crafts-man working in Galatia) had been taken from a captured or dead Turkish officer in one of the famous battles, and records showed it had been at the Vienna Arsenal since 1664.

Partly because of the complexity of the movement and its several calendar and other dials, it had not been disturbed for nearly three centuries. Expert examination at the Vienna War Museum disclosed the surprising fact that the watch must have stopped during the heat of the battle, and the hands were still at 2.30 in the afternoon of the Eighth Muharrem (a Friday) in the year 1045 according to the Mohammedan

Japanese print of foliot-bar clock on a stand.
It is unsigned, but is similar to a roll print by
Shiba Kokan, 1736–1818, of Nagasaki

This Japanese bracket clock has two foliots, operated alternately, to cope with varying lengths of hours by day and night according to the seasons calendar. This gives a mute but vital clue to the date and moment of the historic Battle of the Mohacs, which ended the threat of Turkish invasion of Europe. In Western style the watch indicates 14.30 hours, 1 August 1664.

While in this case the Augsburg-style silver watch is of Turkish manufacture, the vast majority of clocks and watches used by the wealthy in the Ottoman Empire came from a relatively small and exclusive group in London. Their leaders at various periods were George Prior, Markwick Markham, Daniel Evans, George Clarke and Robert Ward.

These men were good clockmakers in their own right, but so considerable did the Turkish trade become that George Prior and others bought up movements or even complete clocks and watches by other makers, and shipped them to the East. This may have been the case with the Markwick family, and certainly was so with George Prior. The two Robert Wards (in London's Abchurch Lane in 1770, and in Plumtree Street, Bloomsbury in 1790) appear always to have signed clocks of their own making. Clocks must have been exported in fair numbers to China and Japan, but due to unusual national and political circumstances Japan was first to set up her own clockmaking industry.

During the period of the Tokugawa dynasty (1600–1868), civil war caused the government to move to Edo (now Tokyo), and foreigners were driven out of the islands. Christianity was suppressed and, so far as clocks were concerned, Japanese craftsmen made a brave attempt to adapt and incorporate the systems first shown to them by the Jesuits and later by Dutch traders.

While the classic Japanese history *Ehon Shomotsu Hajime* refers to a 'time-telling bell' of the Tang dynasty (AD 618–907), it is most unlikely this was more than a temple bell or some device operated by a clepsydra, as in European monasteries.

Japan was discovered by Europe in the early sixteenth century, when Portuguese merchantmen landed there. Jesuits led by St Francis Xavier came to the islands in 1549. Most of the early Japanese clocks extant, as in the examples seen here, were obviously inspired by Continental brass lantern clocks of the period, with a foliot (swinging bar) balance. With the tragic ending of what Rome called 'Japan's Christian century the Japanese élite reverted to the system of timekeeping in which each period from dawn to dusk, through the night until dawn, was separated into six equal divisions. Naturally this meant that at one season of the year when the nights were long, there were six lengthy 'hours' of darkness, and six shorter sessions of day, and the converse at the subsequent season. Thus the hours and minutes were of continually varying duration, according to the season of the year.

This did not present a serious mechanical problem with an escapement of the foliot type, since the positions of the weights on the oscillating bar could be altered to suit. Alternatively, as on the pocket clock seen below on this page, the numerals could be arranged to slide around in a grooved chapter-ring. The owner could thus move six of the numerals closer and the

(*Below*) an *inro* portable clock, attached to the wearer's girdle by its *netsuke* and *ojime*. (*Right*) a mid-19th-century English mantel clock in the Chinese style

others wider apart. With the more costly clocks (as the specimen shown facing p. 108), the movement was fitted with two separate foliot-bars, correctly set for day and night. At dusk and dawn the escapements were automatically changed over, a cam lifting one free from the crown-wheel. The hours were indicated by Chinese numerals, not Japanese, and were given animals' names – Rat, Tiger, Bull, Dragon and so forth.

Clocks made for the Chinese market are so rare that a nineteenth-century quarter-striking clock fetched nearly £2,000 at a famous London auction room. The Chinese style influenced English casemakers, just as it did furniture-makers, in the nineteenth century.

Americana

While the steamboat, the McCormick reaper and the cotton gin were among technical innovations responsible for changing the face of those colonies which were eventually to form the United States, timekeeping took no major part in American development until the mass-production era of the dollar watch.

Unfortunately we know very little today about clocks in the earliest colonial times, although it seems inconceivable that lantern clocks and perhaps even complex table and longcase clocks were not shipped over to the Founding Fathers. In 1629 a request went from New England to Old England for 'such needeful things as every Planter doth or ought to provide'. This list included grain, turkeys, copper kettles, but no clocks. While '$7\frac{1}{2}$ dozen chamber pots, 2s. to 2s. 10d. each', were among the first hardware goods imported by the planters, possibly the setting-up of clocks was difficult in the absence of clockmakers. In time, however, craftsmen came out from Old England; among the first were William Davis (Boston, 1683) and Everardus Bogardus (New Amsterdam, 1698). F. J. Britten indicates that Bogardus was a Freeman of the Company of Clockmakers in London, England.

At the New York Metropolitan Museum, the Chicago Museum, and of course at Henry Ford's fabulous Greenfield Village collection in Dearborn, at what is now part of the Edison Institute, experts have assembled much colonial history. There are few early clocks. The earliest in the Boston Museum of Fine Arts is a longcase clock by William Claggett of Newport, probably no earlier than 1725.

Henry Ford loved history, is misquoted as having said 'History is bunk', and in his own autobiography gives vent to several grass-roots thoughts such as 'It was an evil day when the village flour-mill disappeared'. With an eye for anything mechanical, he would surely have garnered for his beloved Greenfield Village any truly early American clocks. The brass lantern clock hanging in the Cotswold cottage reconstructed at Dearborn is English.

One by one, British clockmaking families went out to the New World, and announced their arrival in the local broadsheets.

From the *New York Mercury*, 3 January 1757: 'Thomas Perry,

(*Above*) the trade card of a 19th-century American clockmaker. (*Right*) a Philadelphia 'Gothic' clock described as an 'improved steel spring eight-day brass clock'

Watch-maker from London, at the sign of the Dial in Hanover Square, makes and cleans all sorts of clocks and watches ... He will import, if bespoke, good warranted clocks, at £14. ...' This was an enormous sum. In the same century, home-built longcase clocks were changing hands for shillings. Perry's shop was in Dock Street, New York City. The *Mercury*, thirty-one years later, proves that 'The Sign of the Dial' was still a clockmaking centre in New York, as one John Ent, a clockmaker there, took new premises in 'the house of Mr John Wright, Watch-maker, in Bayardstreet . . . Gentlemen and Ladies that are pleased to honour him with their Employ may depend on the greatest Care and Dispatch imaginable.'

An Englishman changed this pattern of clockmaking – Thomas Harland, who arrived in Boston in 1773 in the 'teaparty' clipper now enshrined in American history. Harland was not to know that; he had not witnessed the Boston Massacre, and with the independ-

Gilt-wood banjo-style clock by Lemuel Curtis, Concord, Massachusetts, made c. 1815

ent unconcern which affects English shopkeepers in every age, he advertised in *The Norwich Packet* for 9 December 1773: 'Thos. Harland, Watch and Clock-maker from London, Begs leave to acquaint the Publick that he has opened a Shop near the store of Christopher Leffingwell, in Norwich, where he makes in the neatest manner and on the most approved principles, horizontal, repeating and plain watches . . . Clock faces engraved and finished for the trade. Watch wheels and fusees of all sorts and dimensions cut and finished, upon the shortest notice, neat as in London. . . .'

His most distinguished apprentice, Eli Terry, from East Windsor (today South Windsor, Connecticut), became the founder of the American clockmaking industry. In 1793 Terry was making clocks by hand, in the manner taught him by Tom Harland, but within seven years he was diverting the local Niagara Brook across the road to his workshop, and his watch- and clock-making lathes were dri-

(*Above*) American 'Sambo' clock, 1875. (*Below*) an 'Acorn' clock with eight-day movement, 1850

ven by water-power. This was the first clockmaking factory and, as Dr Willis I. Milham the authority on the history of clockmaking in America puts it: 'This is the first small beginning of the tick of the Connecticut clock which was destined to be heard round the world.'

The business was eventually sold to one of his apprentices, Heman Clark, and in 1807–8 Eli Terry opened up a larger business at Greystone, Plymouth, in conjunction with Seth Thomas and Silas Hoadley.

To get them to the public, Terry and others peddled them over much of what today is the great megalopolis stretching from Boston to Washington D.C. and Philadelphia, but most of which then was open country and small townships. Movements sold for $4 each. Local carpenters made the cases, and later the shelf clocks were sold as kits of parts. Terry's thirty-hour clocks had wooden movements, and his 'perfected wooden clock', patented in 1814, earned a fortune for Terry and Seth Thomas. A rival maker, Chauncey Jerome, specializing himself in shelf clocks with brass movements, wrote in his own memoirs of 1860: 'Mr Terry invented a beautiful shelf clock made of wood which completely revolutionized the whole business . . . Mr Terry sold a right to manufacture them to Seth Thomas for one thousand dollars . . . They were sold for $15 a piece when first manufactured. I think that these two men cleared about $100,000 each, up to the year 1825. . . .'

Seth Thomas, Eli Terry and Chauncey Jerome are the three great pioneers of American clockmaking; Simon Willard, Aaron Willard and others linked with his famous family manufactured more decorative and costly clocks in the French fashion, particularly the banjo clock and those with lyre-shaped cases. There is a fine specimen of the latter, by Sawin & Dyer, in the New York Metropolitan Museum of Art, while a decorative banjo in the Anthony Sposato collection, in White Plains, is typical of the fine case-work of this period. Lemuel Curtis, Willard and other makers are the subject of modern reproductions.

Not all the early makers kept their fortunes. In 1855, Chauncey Jerome went bankrupt, partly through an investment in an enterprise of Barnum, the showman and entrepreneur.

Globe mystery clock of the early 19th century

Beauty on the mantel

Because some of the earliest European dwellings at the dawn of the domestic clock were of lath-and-plaster construction, the first chamber clocks were those of the lantern type, hung from a beam by a hook. Trunked longcase clocks could stand on stone floors, and when the great open central brazier gave way to the 'fireplace', with its surrounding mantel, a clock could be placed thereon, or on the sort of walnut sidetable popular in Britain from the Stuart period onwards. As we have seen, the grandeur of some French salons with their rich Boulle-style décor brought the development of very ornate ormolu-decorated clocks.

That a clock should be hung from the wall was a notion which died hard, however, and the fashion for 'bracket' clocks – they could conveniently be supported on a matching bracket hanging from the wall – continued until the nineteenth century. With the passage of time, the majority of the brackets have been mislaid. As owners of clocks moved house, or possessions came to subsequent generations, there was a tendency for spring-wound clocks to be displayed either on the mantelpiece or on a table. Because these were in many instances the clocks that previous owners had kept on brackets, they were still known as bracket clocks.

The terms are used rather loosely by horologists today. Strictly, a bracket clock is one with its original matching bracket, and these are rare. A mantel clock usually has an ornate backplate or other adornment enhancing the clock's appearance when placed against the mirror crowning a mantel-shelf.

The very word 'mantel' is a variant of mantle, derived from the Old French *mantel* and the Latin *mantellum*, meaning a cloak. Mantels surrounding fireplaces were frequently decorated with flowing cloth, as also were bedside tables and dressing-tables. In Victorian times, in Britain, there was a reversion to the type of wood or marble, topped with an 'overmantle' mirror, although in more humble parlours the top of the mantel remained cloth-covered, edged with ball-fringe.

Red lacquer mantel clock by Thomas Turner, made *c.* 1740. It has an eight-day quarter-striking and pull-repeat movement

As we have seen in the preceding section dealing with lantern clocks, the earliest were weight-powered and therefore wound simply by pulling up a rope or chain. A little later they became key-wound, a key being inserted through a hole in the dial-plate and wound in a clockwise direction – that is, in the same direction as the motion of the clock's hands. As seen from the back of the movement, this is in an anti-clockwise direction.

When technological development made the vertical type of table-clock movement possible, there seems to have been no absolute standard. Some early table clocks were wound from the back, and were usually fitted with a plain door, unglazed. This was so with one of the earliest that has survived in England, an ebonized table clock by John Hilderson, a contemporary of Edward East. This maker was not listed initially by Britten, although he mentioned one John Hillersden, a member of the Clockmakers' Company in 1656, which is correct for period. Subsequent research by H. Alan Lloyd brought fresh information on this table-clock maker, and then an important discovery was made of the ebonized clock signed on the back-plate '*John Hilderson in Chessil Street, Londini*'. This is now Chiswell Street, the site of an internationally-famous brewery.

When the Hilderson table clock was made, the maker followed a fashion popular in Continental Europe. The movement was wound by opening an ebonized oak door at the back. Very soon afterwards, the movement was converted to front-wind, through holes in the dial-plate. This may have been because the owner wanted to stand the clock on the now-fashionable mantel, and did not want to take it down each week for winding. Winding from the front, the key has to be turned in an anti-clockwise direction.

Stark ebonized clocks (showing little difference among those in England, Italy and the Low Countries) soon gave way to cases with ornate applied decoration, with chased and gilt mounts, elaborate handles, spires, pierced (cast) basket tops, gilt friezes, capitals and bases. While the Augsburg-style metal-cased clock went out of fashion in England at the end

This mantel pendule by an anonymous Paris clockmaker is in the Empire style, 1800–30

(*Above*) this Swiss calendar-type clock has a thirty-hour movement displaying hours and minutes on ivorine leaves.

(*Opposite*) a rare 19th-century Italian clock by Pasquale Andervelt, powered by hydrogen gas. It is now in the Clockmakers' Company Museum, London

of the sixteenth century, under the influence of the goldsmiths there was a reversion in Stuart times to a table and mantel case style of great richness, the box-like case being of mercurial-gilt brass, of silver, or (more rarely) of bluedsteel. The metal-cased table clock illustrated on p. 47, the gift of Charles II to Barbara, Countess of Castlemaine, is typical of the highest London craftsmanship. These elaborate silver-mounted cases were exported to wealthy patrons in Russia, Spain and elsewhere.

In contrast, British clocks for the table and mantel were usually veneered with pearwood, ebonized, or walnut, king-wood or tortoiseshell.

Towards the end of the seventeenth century, table and mantel clock case makers were swept along with the sudden vogue for 'Indian goods', as all imported Oriental wares were then known.

The East India Company naturally sponsored this interest, and not only were clock cases lacquered ('japanned') in Oriental style, but oak cases were shipped out to Japan to be decorated with lacquer. Cases and other furniture actually made or lacquered in the Orient were known to the trade as 'right Japan'. Broadsheets of the period carried many advertisements, such as this example from *The Daily Courant*, of 12 November 1709: 'The Japan Company will sell all sorts of Lacquer'd Japan and China-Ware, at Garraway's Coffee-house in Exchange-Alley'. This thoroughfare was noted for several London clock-makers.

The fashion died by the middle of the eighteenth century, although as clocks were more costly and complicated than some other articles of furniture, the 'Japand black', 'India Japan' and other clock fashions were tolerated long after mahogany began to dominate the scene for the rest of domestic furniture.

The mantel being the area of main interest in living rooms, there has been an infinite variety of fashions for clocks, ranging from elaborate Boulle-inlaid and ormolu cases to scientific novelties such as the very unusual timepieces seen on pages 122 and 123.

More graceful are mantel clocks in the French taste which began to adorn the mantelshelves of homes throughout Europe until the close of the nineteenth cen-

tury. In France itself they rivalled the cartel (hanging wall clock) and the pedestal clock, although the best examples of the latter were in the Boulle style, almost exclusively French; the cartel case of rococo form, or carved wood or gilt bronze, was rarely seen outside France and Italy.

Rococo 'mantel sets' of matching vases and clock became popular, with gilt brass or polished bronze figures representing characters from the Italian Comedy, or from classic history. Venus, Cupid, *La Nymphe à la Coquille*, lions' heads, Mezzetin with Pantaloon and Pierrot – these were the gay adornments to many a rich French-type mantel clock looking out from the fireplace into a stern Victorian or Germanic 'withdrawing' room.

Some mantel clocks had a musical section in the base – pinned barrels playing tunes on small bells, later a mechanism similar to that of a Swiss comb-type musical box.

French makers pioneered the open-frame *squelette* (skeleton) clock, its delicate brass frame and motion-work open to the gaze but protected by a glass 'shade' or dome. Over 10,000 were sold at London's 1851 Great Exhibition.

Of exquisite design is the 'Fabergé egg' clock seen on the facing page, typical of the European mantel clock at its best. It is of nineteenth-century inspiration, although in fact given as a present in 1903 by the Czar Nicolas II. This clock, the movement of which may have been made in France, was cased by the most outstanding craftsman in Imperial Russia in this type of bijouterie – Carl Fabergé. Of French origin, Fabergé set up Russian workshops in his early twenties, at first in Moscow, later in Odessa, Kiev, and then in London. From a family beginning in 1884, the Russian Imperial family gave egg-shaped jewellery as Easter gifts, symbolizing the Rebirth, and Fabergé's porcelain eggs became internationally sought after. At the peak of his fame he was employing five hundred people in his workrooms. The House of Fabergé continued in London's Bond Street until closed by the First World War in 1915; and it ended in 1918 in Russia, with the start of the Bolshevik regime, terminating an amazing era.

An Easter Egg clock with an enamel case by Carl Fabergé. The cockerel appears at the hour and flaps its diamond-studded wings

Contemporary print of Flamsteed's Octagon Room at the Greenwich Observatory, designed by Sir Christopher Wren in 1675

From the stars

From earliest times, man has charted his course by the stars. At first this was not directly concerned with time as such, but simply with the observation of the position of the sun in day-time, or of the fixed, known stars at night. This gave mariners an indication of their latitude, that is their position north or south of the equator.

No such simple plan could be used for telling a ship's longitude, because of the rotation of the earth and the consequent unknown factor of time. All that a captain could do was to sail a compass course and then allow for the wind and the tide (leeway and drift), working this out by the hit-and-miss process of dead-reckoning. So many mariners' lives were lost that the description 'dead' reckoning became a grim jest.

In 1714 there was a petition to the British Parliament 'that the Discovery of the Longitude is of such Consequence to Great Britain for the safety of the Navy and Merchant Ships . . . that for the want thereof many Ships have been retarded in their Voyages, and many lost. . . .'

Every maritime nation was concerned. King Philip III of

Spain offered a reward of a hundred thousand crowns in 1598 to any man able to ascertain the longitude of a ship at sea. The States General of Holland offered 10,000 florins to the same end. From Venice there came another offer to Italian mathematicians and clockmakers, but to no avail.

Among the several mathematical treatises known in Europe was one by Le Sieur de St Pierre which had been put to Cardinal Richelieu in 1634 and abandoned, partly because of a prior claim by Morin and also because, without some accurate way of telling the time at sea, the scheme could be no more than an astronomical exercise.

The Rev. John Flamsteed, a British astronomer, knew of this St Pierre theory and presented it in London to Charles II, who grudgingly consented to the building of an observatory atop

A photo-zenith tube used to record star transits automatically, as a final correction for caesium-atom 'Uniform Time' clocks

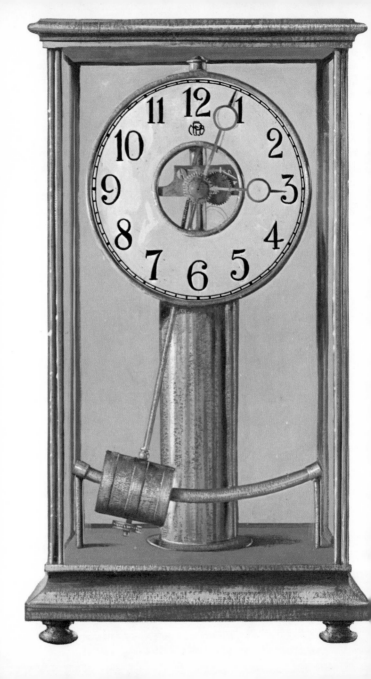

what was then the village of Greenwich, on high ground out-side the City of London. Its purpose was to deal only with this vital problem of determining longitude at sea. The fact that Greenwich Time was to become a world standard could not have been foreseen.

It was decided the cost of the observatory must not exceed £500, this sum being raised by the sale of old gunpowder from Naval stores. Bricks were brought from a demolished fort at Tilbury, and wood from an old gatehouse at the Tower of London.

The warrant of Charles II to his Master of Ordnance, Sir Thomas Chichely, gives no hint of the parsimony attaching to the project. 'Given at Whitehall Court, 4th day of March, 1674. Whereas, in order to the finding out of the longitude of places for perfecting navigation and astronomy, we have resolved to build a small observatory within our park at Greenwich, upon the highest ground, at or near the place where the castle stood, with lodging rooms for our astronomical observator . . . Our will and pleasure is that according to such plot and design as shall be given you by our trusty and well-beloved Sir Christopher Wren, Knight . . . you cause the same to be fenced in, built and finished with all convenient speed. . . .'

Other sites suggested had been Hyde Park and Chelsea, but even in those days the smoke of London made them unsuitable. The first 'astronomical observator' was, wisely, John Flamsteed. Royal shortage of money delayed the practical working of the observatory. Flamsteed had to provide his own instruments from his salary of £100 a year (less £10 annual tax).

Flamsteed had many illustrious successors including Edmond Halley, James Bradley, Nevil Maskelyne, Sir George Airy, Sir Frank Dyson and (in 1933) Sir Harold Spencer-Jones, F.R.S.

Sir Harold, on the occasion of the Tercentenary of Flamsteed's birth in 1946, stated: 'No instruments were ever provided by the Government. His patron Sir Jonas Moore, Surveyor-General of the Ordnance, generously presented him with a large iron sextant, and two clocks by Tompion . . . He

A Bulle electric clock of the 1920s. A 1·5-volt primary cell in the pillar activates the solenoid pendulum also borrowed a small quadrant from the Royal Society, but on the death of Sir Jonas Moore this was called back.

'To meet his expenses it became necessary for him to take private pupils. The King also ordered him to instruct two boys from Christ Church Hospital in mathematics . . . The very books in which observations were entered, the pens and the ink, were all furnished at his own cost. . . .'

Aided by Tompion's clocks, the work was successful. Flamsteed, a young man aged 28, visited Tompion's workshop at Water Lane, off London's Fleet Street, and there were subsequent meetings at Blacklock's coffee-house. Although all contemporary prints show three dials, there were only two clocks. Movements and weights were concealed behind the wainscot, so that the damp Greenwich air should not affect timekeeping. It did, however. Flamsteed proudly recorded: 'My Pendulum clocks were the work of Mr Tompion. The pendulums, 13 feet long, make each single vibration in two seconds of time. Their weights need to be drawn up only once in twelve months.' But when mechanical trouble developed,

Regate Aquastar watch dial display, used for timing yacht races

Pul-syn-etic automatic ship position indicator, developed at the beginning of the 20th century. The ship's time system controls a pilot model on the map

Flamsteed complained: 'One of our clocks goes well: the other may be made to doe so too if Mr Tompion could be prevailed with to come & bestow a little Paines upon it. . . .'

Meanwhile, the imaginary line known as the meridian of longitude was taken as passing through Greenwich, and this became known as the 'prime meridian' from which longitude is measured east or west. If one assumes that the earth rotates completely once every twenty-four hours, then each hour represents fifteen degrees, or one degree every four minutes. Provided Greenwich time is known aboard ship, it is a simple matter to determine the longitude.

Sir Isaac Newton, called in 1714 to report to a Parliamentary committee, said that what was needed was a watch to keep time exactly, '. . . but by reason of the Motion of the Ship at Sea, the Variation of Heat and Cold, Wet and Dry, and the

This Mercer survey chronometer, giving accuracy to a one-hundredth of a second, is used in cartography to check points by radio astro-observations

Difference of Gravity in different latitudes, such a Watch has not yet been made'.

Queen Anne approved a Parliamentary plan to set up twenty-two judges, 'Commissioners of the Board of Longitude', with power to award the enormous sum of £20,000 if a suitable marine watch could be developed, capable of making calculation of longitude possible to within an error of thirty miles on a voyage to the West Indies, at least six weeks at sea. It has been calculated that the award would be worth £100,000 (a quarter of a million dollars) nowadays and, as was only to be expected, the Commissioners were not over-eager to pay it.

The clockmaker John Harrison spent thirty years of his life in this quest, and saw several sea trials. On one of them the

Astronomer Royal Nevil Maskelyne sailed in HMS *Princess Louisa* to Barbados. An award of £10,000 was eventually made to Harrison, and after many years' wrangling the final sum was paid, following a petition to Parliament.

In the following years the British Government offered further sums of up to £10,000 for a marine timepiece determining longitude to within half a degree.

There were many contenders, including the London chronometer and watchmakers Thomas Mudge, John Arnold and Thomas Earnshaw. Arnold was first in the field, and his No. 3 chronometer was tested on *Resolution* during Captain Cook's second voyage. Arnold was already a famous watchmaker, having received an award of 500 guineas from George III for a small quarter-repeater watch set in a ring, the movement only one-third of an inch in diameter. He refused an offer of a thousand guineas to make a duplicate for the Empress of Russia.

Claims of all contenders in the quest for longitude were examined, and Arnold, Earnshaw and Mudge were paid £3,000 each.

A synchronous clock mechanism is buried in the centre of this floral clock. which has an 18-foot dial display

Big Ben

One of the most famous clocks of all time is the Great Clock at Westminster above the British Houses of Parliament, known internationally but incorrectly as 'Big Ben'. This is the nickname given to the huge hour-bell, not the clock movement, after the Chief Commissioner Sir Benjamin Hall (later Lord Llanover) responsible for directing the work of building the new Palace of Westminster following the disastrous fire in 1834. All that was left standing, then, was the historic Westminster Hall (today an integral part of the Palace of Westminster) which had existed in the time of Canute, and was used by Edward the Confessor and William the Conqueror.

'Big Ben' was not the first clock at the Palace of Westminster. There had been a clock in the courtyard at Westminster in 1386, in the reign of Edward III. The keeper of it, one John Nicole, was paid sixpence a day. In early Royal rolls there are references to this *horologii Regis infra palatium Westm.*'

After the 1834 fire, the architect Sir Charles Barry was commissioned to design a new building to house the Houses of Lords and Commons. Ultimately this was to cost over £2,100,000. It was obvious there should be an exceptional clock to adorn the tower, and Barry wrote to the distinguished clockmaker Benjamin Louis Vulliamy, clockmaker to Queen Victoria and member of a family of Swiss origin.

'I shall be obliged,' he said, 'by your informing me whether you would be disposed to furnish me with a plan for the clock . . . I propose that this clock should strike the hours on a bell of from eight to ten tons, and show the time upon four dials about 30 feet in diameter. . . .'

Vulliamy offered to build 'the most powerful eight-day clock ever made in this country', but there were offers from other directions and the 'Commissioners of her Majesty's Woods and Forests' began to regret that the whole project had not been competitive from the outset.

The assistance was sought of the Astronomer Royal, Sir George Airy. He proposed a specification which included the condition that the movement of this turret clock should be capable of maintaining an accuracy of under one second at the bell's first stroke each hour. Although the firms of Vulliamy, E. J. Dent and Whitehurst (of Derby) were all established

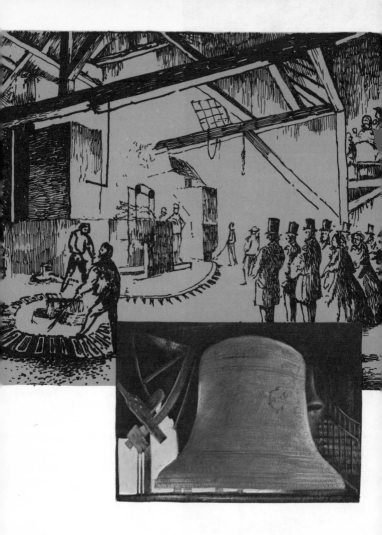

The thirteen-and-a-half ton hour bell of the Palace of Westminster clock, nicknamed 'Big Ben' after Sir Benjamin Hall, who was in charge of the construction of the new Palace after the fire of 1834. Few who hear Big Ben on radio and television know that it still has the flaw made in it during its initial sounding tests when the 750-pound clapper cracked the bell

builders of turret clocks, such a degree of accuracy had never been attained, chiefly because of the enormous variations of wind-pressure on large clock-hands. Vulliamy withdrew from the contest and did not tender. Whitehurst put in a tender of just over £3,000, but Dents were prepared to build a first-rate clock for only £1,500 because of the prestige which would result.

E. J. Dent died during the ensuing disputes, with the clock not completed. A further dispute arose as to whether his stepson Frederick Dent was entitled to take over the contract, which by now had been reassessed at £1,800. Under pressure from the Astronomer Royal, the distinguished barrister and amateur scientist Edmund Denison, M.A., Q.C., joined the design team. Denison was a man of tremendous energy and initiative, and, among many interests, was the author of a textbook on watch and clockmaking. He pioneered a form of gravity

Today, the Westminster clock is world-famous

The movement of the Palace of Westminster clock, said to be 'the most accurate clock in the world'

('free') escapement keeping the pendulum free from external influences such as wind-pressure or rain or ice on the hands.

This movement, largely planned by Denison and built by Dents, was put in hand in 1852 and completed within two years, but was not installed in the Palace tower for a further five years.

Because of disputes, the Astronomer Royal resigned from his post as one of the timekeeping referees, and the Board of Works also tried to force Denison to resign. Ultimately he won the day, and in 1886 was rewarded by being raised to the peerage, with the title of Baron Grimthorpe. His famous escapement was copied by other builders of turret movements. It was even reproduced in miniature on a few rare occasions, and fitted into longcases so that private horologists could see it functioning. One of these is in the author's collection today. The same gravity escapement can be seen in the illustration

View behind one of the four huge dials of the Palace of Westminster clock, which are illuminated electrically at night. The minute-hands are 14 feet long

above, of the 'Big Ben' movement itself.

The present bell is the second to hang in the tower. When the first was cast it weighed sixteen tons (two tons more than the estimate), so was too heavy for rail transport. It had to be brought from the Stockton-on-Tees foundry by ship, broke loose from its deck moorings, and when finally put in wooden gallows at Westminster it cracked on the first stroke of the clapper. It was then taken in pieces to a Whitechapel foundry which had cast Bow Bells, refounded perfectly at a weight of thirteen-and-a-half tons, and eventually inched up into the tower. The four quarter bells were those from the Stockton foundry, and the total bill was £6,000.

Founders warned that the clapper should not exceed 450 pounds, but Denison insisted on a larger one. On the first blow a minute crack appeared in the bell. It is still there, although

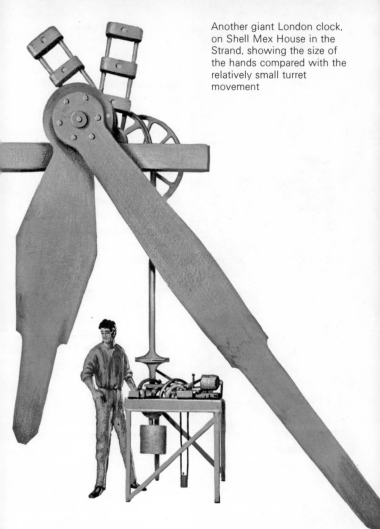

Another giant London clock, on Shell Mex House in the Strand, showing the size of the hands compared with the relatively small turret movement

the E-natural rings true. A slot has been cut in the bell lip to prevent the crack from spreading. The four quarter chimes are G, B, E and F, and the fashion has grown for believing that they chime out: 'All through this hour, Lord be my Guide. And by Thy power, No foot shall slide.'

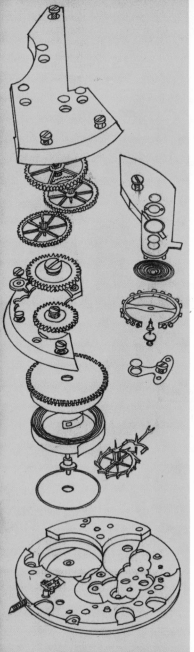

Modern watches

World production of watches is dominated by the Swiss watchmaking industry. In one typical year some 67,000,000 watches were produced in Switzerland and exported all over the world, bringing little Switzerland a gross revenue of about £250,000,000, or $600,000,000.

Although currently there is American development by the Hamilton group and parallel research in Japan into techniques of producing completely all-electrical watches with no moving parts at all (using a crystal oscillator and static fluorescent dial display), the leading electronic balance-wheel watches are produced by a Geneva group. Further, the outstanding electronic Accutron was developed in Switzerland by Max Hetzel and produced by the Bulova Watch Company.

One reason for this domination is, of course, the importance of watchmaking to the Swiss national exchequer, and the consequent legal statutes maintaining an extremely high standard of production and testing. In 1962 the offi-

Exploded view of a modern
Swiss jewelled lever
watch, with 127 parts

cial body known as the 'FH' (*Federation des associations de fabricants suisses d'Horlogerie*) set up an authority known as the 'CTM' (*Controle technique suisse des montres*) which compels manufacturers to produce only watches that will maintain the high Swiss standard in other countries. It also tests representative samples off production-lines. This body has its headquarters at Neuchâtel, and its expenses are covered by a tax on export permits, by the Swiss Chamber of Watchmaking.

The drawings on the two pages here show how this 400-year-old craft has been developed in the conventional spring-driven watch.

In the movement of a typical lady's small Swiss watch, 127 separate components fit into about as much space as one-

A typical Smiths Industries watch, showing (*left*) balance, hairspring, lever and escape-wheel and (*right*) mainspring

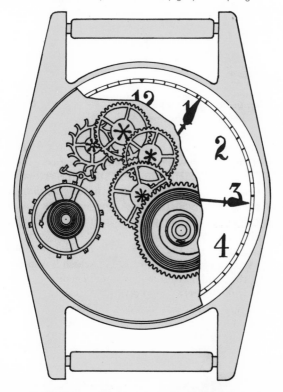

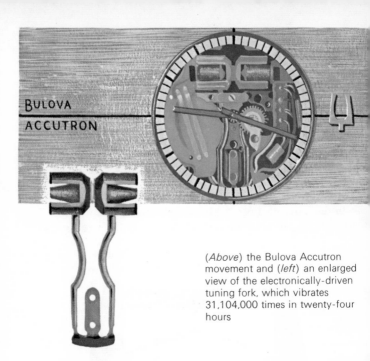

(*Above*) the Bulova Accutron movement and (*left*) an enlarged view of the electronically-driven tuning fork, which vibrates 31,104,000 times in twenty-four hours

sixth of an ordinary lump of sugar. These include 19 wheels, 42 screws, jewels and springs.

When the case is opened at the back, the only moving parts that can be seen are the balance-wheel, spring, and a very small section of the jewelled escapement. The tiny T-shaped jewelled lever alternately stops and starts the escape-wheel, releasing one tooth at a time. The lever in turn is controlled by the balance-wheel oscillating back and forth. As this wheel swings it tightens the hairspring, which then gives it an impulse in the opposite direction.

The rate at which the balance-wheel oscillates depends upon the type of watch and purpose for which it is to be used. Currently the tendency is towards movements with faster-running balance-wheels, but in general one expects to find the watch ticking every fifth of a second. This means the unit of time 'escaped' by this portion of the movement is one fifth of a second, or 1/432,000th of a day. If the watch is to have a good rate, the wheel must oscillate as nearly as possible to 432,000 times every twenty-four hours.

While the casual wearer may believe that the component which has the most strain is the mainspring, in fact one of the most stressed components is the balance-staff, the shaft and pivots carrying the balance-wheel. The tips of the balance-staff are fitted into very hard-wearing jewelled bearings. Microscopic oil cups reduce wear and friction. Teeth of wheels and pinions in a watch movement must match precisely, to avoid friction and to secure a good rate. Gear-wheels in automobiles are ground to obtain smooth running, but some watch parts are machined to tolerances of two or three microns (one micron equals about thirty-nine millionths of an inch), and components are assembled under a microscope.

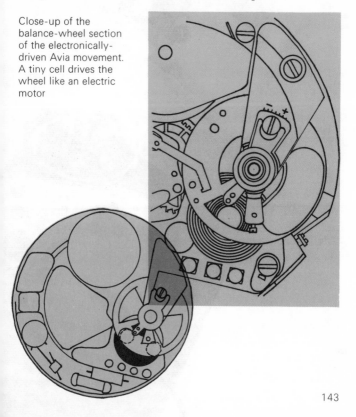

Close-up of the balance-wheel section of the electronically-driven Avia movement. A tiny cell drives the wheel like an electric motor

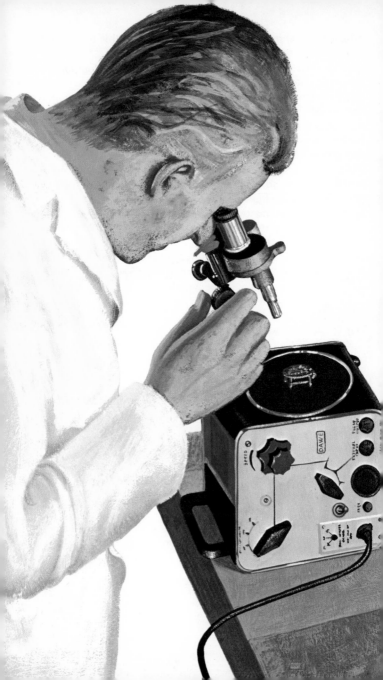

In a lady's watch some hairsprings are extremely small, down to thirteen hundredths of an inch in diameter. The spring must be extremely hard yet possess a high degree of elasticity, and also be immune to temperature change. Hairsprings are made from special nickel alloys containing chromium, beryllium, titanium or tungsten.

They pulsate one-and-a-half million times every week in a watch with a conventional escapement, so of course the slightest variation through temperature, humidity, magnetic or other external influence will affect the rate. To this must be added the variation in tension of the mainspring. All these components are handling considerable force and withstanding unexpected wear. In a watch in which the balance-wheel makes 120,000,000 oscillations every nine months, this is roughly the equivalent of an automobile's road-wheels after 160,000 miles.

Self-winding watches, in which the mainspring is kept fairly constantly wound by means of an oscillating-weight mechanism, keep a good rate, since the mainspring power is steady. Many other systems are used to achieve an even better rate. In the electronic watch of the Avia type, for example, there is a fairly conventional balance-wheel and wheel-train, but instead of powering the movement by a mainspring, a small dry cell is used to oscillate the balance-wheel electrically.

A completely different system is used in the Accutron, pioneered in the Bulova plant at Bienne, Switzerland. The Bulova Watch Company grew from a small jewellery shop in 1875, and today has eleven factories in different parts of the world. In the Bulova Accutron, a small mercury cell powers an oscillatory circuit which vibrates a tuning fork at a frequency of 360 times a second. This drives the hands through an indexing wheel. In place of the twenty-three moving parts of a spring-driven automatic watch, the Accutron has only twelve. The high rate of vibrations—31,104,000 a day—reduces practically to zero the effect of outside influences.

As the indexing wheel of the Accutron is impulsed 360 times every second, a Dawe Stroboflash is used to give an operator the stroboscopic impression the mechanism is stationary, so that it can be adjusted.

Time for sale

Good clocks and watches, like all fine mechanisms, have always cost a good deal of money. It is, of course, difficult to state the exact modern equivalent of the 500 guineas awarded to John Arnold in 1764 for George III's tiny ring watch. In those days Arnold charged 25 guineas for his cheapest silver-cased watches, and about 80 guineas for a marine chronometer. Earlier, in the 1690s, Thomas Tompion charged £40 for a tortoiseshell mantel clock, and £70 for a gold repeating watch. So highly were these items valued that newspapers advertised rewards up to £30 (then a very considerable sum) for the return of stolen watches. This was in the era when best silver cost 6s. 2d. an ounce.

Moving to the nineteenth century, A.-L. Breguet in Paris charged the Princess Murat 3,300 francs for a quarter-repeating watch, and an even higher amount of 6,000 francs to one Colonel Hervey for a watch with a more intricate movement.

By the dawn of the twentieth century, old things were starting to be appreciated as *objets d'art*. As clocks and watches were ranged along with antique silver, glass and porcelain, their values rose rapidly in the world's salerooms.

A striking example was given by the art expert W. E. Hurcomb who handled some of the largest clock sales at that period. He told of a certain nobleman in Berkeley Square who had sold £300-worth of junk to a dealer who stored it in Soho, where it was sold by auction. A Tompion longcase clock changed hands for 27s. Hurcomb bought it for £8, propped it up in a hansom-cab and passed it on to a distinguished Lombard Street banker.

Major sales of horological antiquities are held in London at auction rooms such as those of Christie and Sotheby, to which many European buyers come; and in the United States at centres such as the Parke-Bernet Galleries or the various 'Sotheby's of London' companies in Texas, California and elsewhere. They commenced with Baker, Leigh & Sotheby in 1744.

Rival rooms were opened in 1766, in Pall Mall, London, by James Christie when he was only 33. He was dubbed by

A clock sale in a London auction rooms. Today, antique clocks rank in sale value with other great works of art

cartoonists 'The Specious Orator', and it is said he would invite bidding in an opening sentence such as: 'Ladies and gentlemen, permit me to put this inestimable piece of elegance under your protection; only observe, the inexhaustible munificence of your candid generosity must harmonize with the refulgent brilliancy of this little jewel. . . .'

The first important sale featuring clocks took place at Christie's in 1904, when effects of the Duke of Cambridge were sold. An old longcase clock left behind in one of the bedrooms was turned out hastily, catalogued in two lines, and sold for 125 guineas. In 1911 it reappeared at Christie's and went for 380 guineas. It was, in fact, the gem of the Dunn collection of clocks, a three-month Tompion clock bearing the monogram of William III, and formerly at Hampton Court. In later years this clock commanded a fortune, and crossed the Atlantic more than once to various owners.

In May 1928, Mr Hurcomb handled at one memorable sale

Soltronic electric clock with no moving mechanical components. The time element is a quartz crystal, and the time is indicated by fluorescent radial bars

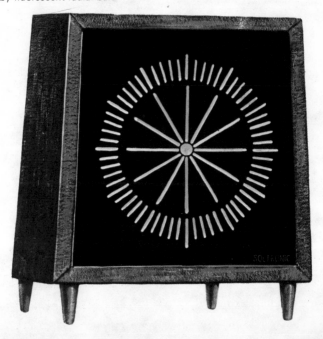

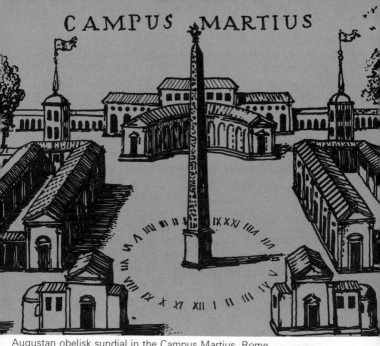

CAMPUS MARTIUS

Augustan obelisk sundial in the Campus Martius, Rome

222 clocks for a total of £30,000. This was the entire collection of David E. F. Wetherfield. It has been dispersed through the years to many other distinguished collections. At one period an outstanding ex-Wetherfield clock (the thirty-hour Tompion shown on p. 77) changed hands for around $25,000.

Appreciation of values through the years is not constant, but depends upon facts such as the world economic situation. In 1968 the two Breguet watches mentioned (sold to the Princess Murat and Colonel Hervey) were auctioned at Sotheby's for £2,700 and £6,200 (nearly $15,000) respectively. Yet when the world situation worsened early in 1970, several Breguet watches auctioned at the same rooms fetched less than £1,000 each.

Apart from recognized trade values, prices are dictated to some extent by collector's interest, in Britain by members of the Antiquarian Horological Society, and in the United States by the National Association of Watch and Clock Collectors.

Split-second time

Nowadays civilization depends not upon the simple matter of telling the time, but is dominated by time. Nation-wide electric power networks carry electricity alternating at precisely 50 cycles (in Europe) or 60 cycles (in the United States and elsewhere) per second.

Frequency-constancy is not important for light and heat, within certain limits affecting power capability, but it is vital for intricate electronic circuitry in industry and in television, and of course for electric clocks. They are virtually AC (alternating current) motors depending upon getting fifty or sixty alternations every second to indicate sixty seconds in the hour.

Nation-wide television networks feed millions of receivers which are 'sync'd' (synchronized) to the public mains supplies so that each of the picture-frames may be produced on the screen from the transmitted signal – fifty or sixty frames per second – and in turn each frame is scanned with lines (525 in the United States, and 405 and 625 lines in Britain), with the timing of the start of each line regulated to a minute fraction of a second.

The heart of these precise electronic timekeepers is the 'sync pulse generator', a unit quite independent of mains frequency. It generates a basic oscillation related to the video frequency needed, and this is stepped up by selecting harmonics. The source of the oscillations may be a quartz crystal, with the first stages housed in a temperature-regulated oven for stability, but currently even greater stability is obtained from generators using silicon transistors.

Precise timing is vital for computers and data transmission, and for colour television. The video section of a colour-TV broadcast does not use three separate channels for the basic red, green and blue which the camera tubes handle. Separate signals are handled over a common channel, separated by intervals of time in what is known as a phase-difference.

To obtain a satisfactory colouring, the chrominance signal phase errors have to be kept down to fractions of a nanosecond, that is a unit of one thousand-millionth (10^9) of a second. Any serious difference in phase changes the hue of the picture.

When dealing with such extremely brief time-intervals,

engineers must consider even the speed of waveforms along a cable. The length of the camera cable itself can be critical, since a cable of 30 metres (about 33 feet) can produce a delay of 50 nanoseconds. Resistance-capacity circuits are introduced to equalize time delays of this sort, never dreamed of by early clock or chronometer builders.

Until January 1965, Greenwich Mean Time (GMT) was the basic world standard. Originally, as we have seen, the line of longitude at Greenwich was accepted as the prime meridian of the world. As international marine competition grew, it became necessary to call an international conference to agree this 'longitude zero'. At this meeting in 1884, France and

Electronic timekeeping accuracy to $2\frac{1}{2}$ parts in a million is required to network national television transmitters

Ireland dissented, although seventy-two per cent of the world's shipping tonnage already had the Greenwich meridian on their charts, and even the North American railroad network used GMT as a basis. However, until 1916 the Irish insisted upon keeping 'Dublin time', and the Paris Observatory decided upon a time-difference of 9 minutes 21 seconds.

There was an innovation in domestic timekeeping in 1924 when the British Broadcasting Company (later Corporation) commenced broadcasting the famous six-pip time signals. A tube (valve) oscillator was used to create the tone, and the transmission was controlled from Greenwich. The pips were spaced at one-second intervals, the final sixth pip giving the exact time. With the 'Big Ben' broadcasts, the first stroke indicates the hour.

While this was satisfactory for domestic timekeeping, it was not precise enough for navigation. World-wide time signals were transmitted on short waves by the BBC, and the British Post Office and other telecommunications authorities in other countries started the 'TIM' telephone talking clocks (from London on 24 July 1936). But a better standard was needed for navigational and scientific purposes.

Due to irregularities in the earth's rotation, the exact point of zero meridian changes. There is a further movement of the earth's axis known as mutation. In 1950 a Universal Time conference was called, and compensation for all known variations agreed. 'Uniform Time' came into operation in 1965, in readiness for satellite communication and space travel, both of which demand a high accuracy rate and a firm world standard.

Tompion's clocks at Greenwich Observatory showed an accuracy no better than ten seconds a day. Precision astronomical clocks (some protected in airtight cases) were developed by Leroy & Cie, Clemens Riefler, E. Dent & Co. and others. Greenwich had its first electric clock in 1852, and this had a daily accuracy of about 0·3 seconds. The atomic clocks used nowadays show an accuracy of much better than one millionth of a second a day. Observations now made by the Royal Observatory at Herstmonceux, in Sussex, make allowance for the difference in longitude compared with Greenwich.

The world's first operational atomic clock (correctly known

Quartz-crystal clocks with digital display (*below*) are used to time record-breaking attempts by cars, boats, aircraft and missiles

as the atomic frequency standard) was designed and built in Britain, at the National Physical Laboratory where some of the world's first work on that other important British invention, radar, was started. The atomic frequency standard has been running since June 1955.

It measures time with an accuracy of one part in ten thousand million, 0·000001 second a day, one second in 300 years. The caesium atom is used as a basis, since this can exist in two states. Transition from one to the other radiates energy at a fixed frequency. This controls the timekeeping. A beam of caesium atoms is emitted in a highly evacuated tube, between two focussing magnets and a radio-frequency magnetic field. When the frequency of this field equals the atomic frequency, atoms pass to a detector at the other end of the tube. When the stream of atoms is at the maximum, the radio-frequency oscillator is operating at the atomic frequency. This oscillator then calibrates further oscillators, and/or can display on a dial or read-out device. The atomic standard itself is checked by time-markers from astronomical time. Regular checks are made on the stars, using a photo-zenith tube of the type seen on p. 127. This automatically corrects for human observation errors, and in turn is controlled by each observatory's quartz-crystal clock.

Need for precise time accuracy on the Uniform Time standard became obvious when the Apollo and other series of space probes and missions began.

The National Aeronautics and Space Administration (NASA) set up on behalf of all those concerned with the United States' projects a communication network across the world, and each station on the network is in time-step. Switching centre for this network is at Goddard, under NASA control, with secondary switching centres at Canberra, Madrid, London, Honolulu, Hawaii, Guam and Cape Kennedy. Part of this world time and communications link is by space satellite. Data is transmitted at 2,400 bits per second from Cape Kennedy, and increased to 40,800 bits per second to Houston.

In the project to get men to Mars, very exact timekeeping has been involved, and the atomic frequency standard check tells us that the rotation speed of Mars is 24 hours 37 minutes and 22·6679 seconds precisely.

(*Below*) a section of the Mission Control rooms at Houston, Texas, showing some of the electronic time-display screens

GLOSSARY

Anchor: escapement with toothed escape wheel and pallets shaped like anchor flukes.

Arbor: Spindles on which clock wheels are fixed.

Balance wheel: single-spoked wheel, usually of iron or brass, oscillated by a toothed crown-wheel.

Chapter-ring: hour-ring on which the minute and hour indications are engraved or painted, in Roman (early) or Arabic (late) numerals.

Collet: Washer or boss, usually employed to keep clock-hands in place.

Crown-wheel: Toothed train-wheel in the escapement, so-called because the position of its teeth resembles the raised edge of a crown.

Dead-beat escapement: Like the anchor escapement, but with teeth and pallets so arranged that there is a sliding action, without recoil as in the anchor.

Escapement: The final section of the train of a clock or watch. It allows the power of the weight or spring to 'escape' slowly, a fraction of a second at a time.

Grand Sonnerie: System of striking in which the quarters are sounded, then the preceding or nearest hour sounded on another bell.

Hood: The top section of a longcase clock.

Lenticle: Glazed opening, oval or circular, in the trunk door of a longcase clock, showing the pendulum bob.

Locking-plate striking: Disc or wheel in the striking train (external in the earliest clocks), notched to take a lifting-piece which 'counts the hours'. Also known as the count-wheel.

Movement: The mechanical heart of a clock or watch, usually misdescribed as the 'works'.

Rack striking: System of striking first applied by Tompion, using a toothed rack with a lifting-piece to count the hours.

Repeater: Striking mechanism which can be tripped off by pulling a cord (clocks) or pressing a button (watches) to sound the hours, quarters or minutes.

Regulator: Precision clock, used as time standard.

Skeleton dial: Chapter-ring cut away between Roman numerals to show matted or tooled dial-plate.

Spandrels: Decorative cast corner pieces on dial-plate.

Trunk: The body of a longcase clock.

BOOKS TO READ

Among the many books written about clocks and watches, the following are generally available from publishers or bookshops, or through public libraries.

British Clocks and Clockmakers by Kenneth Ullyett. Collins, London, 1947.

British Time by D. de Carle. Crosby Lockwood, 1947.

Clocks by Simon Fleet. Weidenfeld and Nicolson, London, 1961.

Clocks by Edward T. Joy. Country Life, London, 1967.

Clocks and Watches by Eric Bruton. Hamlyn, London, 1968.

The Collector's Dictionary of Clocks by H. Alan Lloyd. Country Life, London, 1964.

English Domestic Clocks by H. Cescinsky and M. R. Webster. Reprinted from the 1913 edition by Spring Books, London, 1969.

The First Twelve Years of the English Pendulum Clock by Ronald A. Lee. Privately published, 1969.

French Clocks by Winthrop Edey. Studio Vista, London, 1967.

In Quest of Clocks by Kenneth Ullyett. Spring Books, London, 1968.

John Harrison by Humphrey Quill. John Baker, London, 1966.

Klokken by W. F. J. Hana. Uitgeversmaatschappij C. A. J. van Dishoeck, 1963.

La Pendule Française by Tardy. Paris, 1964.

The Plain Man's Guide to Antique Clocks by W. J. Bentley. Michael Joseph, London, 1963.

Technique and History of the Swiss Watch by E. Jaquet and A. Chapuis. Revised edition, Spring Books, London, 1970.

Thomas Tompion by R. W. Symonds. Reprinted from the 1951 edition by Spring Books, London, 1969.

Time and Timekeepers by Willis I. Milham. Macmillan, London, 1941.

Timekeepers by F. A. B. Ward. Her Majesty's Stationery Office, London, 1963.

Watch Collecting by Kenneth Ullyett. Muller, London, 1970.

Watches by T. P. Camerer Cuss. Country Life, London, 1967.

INDEX

SOME OTHER TITLES IN THIS SERIES

Natural History

The Animal Kingdom
Animals of Australia & New Zealand
Animals of South America
Animals of Southern Asia
Bird Behaviour
Birds of Prey

Butterflies
Evolution of Life
Fishes of the World
Fossil Man
A Guide to the Seashore

Gardening

Chrysanthemums

Garden Flowers

Popular Science

Astronomy
Atomic Energy
Computers at Work

The Earth
Electricity
Electronics

Arts

Architecture
Glass

Jewellery

General Information

Arms and Armour
Coins and Medals
Flags

Guns
Military Uniforms
Rockets and Missiles

Domestic Animals & Pets

Budgerigars
Cats

Dog Care
Dogs

Domestic Science

Flower Arranging

History & Mythology

Archaeology
Discovery of
    Africa
    Australia
    Japan

Discovery of
    North America
    South America
    The American West